G O D

B R E A T H E D

BREATHED

THE UNDENIABLE POWER and RELIABILITY of SCRIPTURE

Josh McDowell

SHILOH RUN  PRESS

An Imprint of Barbour Publishing, Inc.

Print ISBN 978-1-63058-941-7

eBook Editions:
Adobe Digital Edition (.epub) 978-1-63409-381-1
Kindle and MobiPocket Edition (.prc) 978-1-63409-382-8

Member of the
Evangelical Christian
Publishers Association

Printed in Canada.

Contents

Acknowledgments

I wish to recognize the following individuals for their valuable contributions to this book.

Dave Bellis, my friend and colleague for thirty-eight years, for collaborating with me on the outline of the book, pulling from my talks and other works to then write the first draft, folding in all the edits, and shaping this work into its final form. I recognize Dave's insights and writing skills, and I'm deeply grateful for his contribution.

Tom Williams, for editing the manuscript, to which he applied his valuable insights, wordsmithing skills, and passionate heart to help make these words come alive on the printed page.

Becky Bellis, for laboring at the computer to ready the manuscript.

Don and Judy Kencke, for reviewing the manuscript and providing insightful guidance.

Dave Lindstedt, for the editorial guidance he brought to the manuscript's completion.

Kelly McIntosh, vice president of editorial at Barbour Publishing, and managing editor Annie Tipton, for their expert insights and help in shaping the outline of the book.

Tim Martins, president of Barbour Publishing, and the entire Barbour Publishing team, who caught the vision for *God-Breathed* and labored tirelessly to bring this book to reality.

Josh McDowell

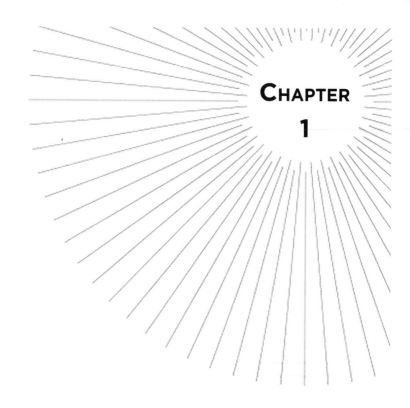

CHAPTER 1

What's in a Word?

Nineteen years old and quite a skeptic. That described me as I left college and traveled to Europe to do research in an attempt to disprove Christianity—specifically to show that the Bible was historically unreliable and that Jesus was by no means the Son of God.

Standing in the Glasgow University library in Scotland, I stared at an ancient New Testament manuscript. It was a fragment from John 16, and the ink and papery substance on which it was written were more than sixteen hundred years old. This rare, third-century, handwritten portion of the Gospel of John was housed under a protective glass case in the university library. It was a priceless artifact that quoted the words of Jesus.

As I stood there, a strange and unexpected feeling washed over me. Though I could not read or understand a single line of the Greek in which that manuscript was written, those words seemed to reach out to me in an almost mystical way. Even though I was an unbeliever at the time, I sensed an uncanny power about those words.

Today's Noisy Words

Words. The right ones used in the right way can be powerful. But in today's world, I'm afraid a lot of people use a lot of words to produce merely a lot of noise.

Everywhere you look, you see people using a barrage of words in bite-size chunks in hopes of communicating. Take texting, for example. Our generation is "connected" now more than ever by smartphones. According to a recent Experian Marketing Services digital marketer report, the average number of texts per month by eighteen- to twenty-four-year-olds is 3,853. That is more than 128 texts a day.[1]

People are using words at an unprecedented rate through Facebook as well. Within the first quarter of 2014, Facebook reported more than 1.15 billion active users per month.[2] The market research company eMarketer estimates that 40 percent of all US children under the age of twelve are online monthly. Nearly half will be online by 2015.[3]

It's clear in today's world of texts, Twitter, Facebook, and e-mails that we are transmitting words at record levels. But are all these words truly *connecting* us, or are many of them simply a lot of noise? The Creator of words had a purpose in mind when he gave us the ability to write words and speak them to others. Used properly, words can effectively connect us relationally. Words are important, and the God-breathed words of Scripture are the most important of all. But we must *listen* to how words are being used in order to understand their true meaning.

Listening for the Meaning of Words

We humans have the unique ability to make varied sounds and arrange them in specific combinations that we call words. And each of these words is designed to mean something in particular. The languages we speak are composed of words, which are the building blocks of thoughts, ideas, and expressed feelings. When we assemble words in sentences to represent our thoughts, ideas, and feelings, they become the basic elements of our human communication.

Using words enables us to accomplish much of what we do in life. Through words we can communicate how to get from one place to another, complete tasks, form friendships, express love to a spouse, raise a family, and express our views on countless subjects. Words can transmit creative thoughts and ingenious ideas, but their most meaningful purpose is when we use them to connect to one another relationally. Yet when we're not attentive to words, or we fail to listen carefully to what someone says, words can become mere sounds or marks on a page and lose their power to connect us.

I remember the tragic beginning of my honeymoon. Dottie and I had known each other for only six short months before we married. I figured my lovely wife and I had a lifetime to really get to know each other, so I was in no particular hurry to discover all there was to know about her. But that wasn't the case for my new bride. I soon discovered that she was anxious to share her entire life story with me on our honeymoon.

We were driving a long distance through Mexico to Acapulco when Dottie began to tell me about herself, her family, her childhood, her likes and dislikes, her views on politics, marriage, and child rearing. You name it, and Dottie was prepared to talk about it.

I remember that, at some point, my receptive facilities went into overload and all the words she was saying began to sound like mere noise. Meanwhile, I was also trying to interpret the confusing road signs and stopping occasionally to fumble with a stack of maps. After a while, Dottie's talking became intermittent, and eventually she became silent. During that whole time, I had said little except the occasional "Yeah," "Uh-huh," and "I see." But to be honest, I got practically nothing out of my new wife's marathon of words. In fact, I hardly even noticed when she stopped talking.

Dottie had used a lot of words, but they meant little to me and did nothing to bring us closer together. Of course, she hadn't felt the need to explain to me what should have been obvious—that her exercise in self-disclosure was simply so that her brand-new husband could better know his brand-new wife. But when it became clear that I was clueless to what she was trying to accomplish, Dottie didn't remain shut down for long. She blew up!

It wasn't the best start to a honeymoon, but after Dottie explained what she was trying to do, and I did a lot of apologizing, we figured it out together. From that point on, our words began to make sense to one another. I began to see the loving heart of my wife, who wanted me to know her for who she is, and she began to see a husband who, despite his initial lapse into insensitivity, wanted to make his new wife happy.

As Dottie and I look back at our honeymoon now, we laugh about it. But it taught us the importance of words and of listening and interpreting and finding the true meaning of thoughts and feelings that flow from our hearts.

It takes time and effort to communicate effectively with meaningful words. It also takes time and effort to listen, translate, and accurately interpret the meaning of those words. In a real sense, there is an art to using words. And the God-breathed words of Scripture, in particular, artfully communicate a powerful message designed to bring meaning to our lives.

God Is the Master of Powerful Words

"God said, 'Let there be. . .'" (Genesis 1:3). At some point in the distant past, God spoke words. And when he did, things happened. There was such creative power behind those words that the sun, stars, and moon burst into being. Out of God's mouth came words that formed everything that exists, including you and me.

Not only did God use powerful words to bring about the existence of all things, he also used words to bring meaning to our lives and our relationships. Then, in time, he had those meaningful words committed to writing.

The Bible, God-breathed words of life, is meant to give us everything we need in order to understand who we are, why we're here, and where we're going. It is made up of living words from God himself to guide us to the very meaning of life, love, relationships, and the joy God originally intended for his children. The words in the Bible are extremely powerful. Yet, for whatever reason, far too many people in the world have failed to be gripped by the power of those words.

In the pages of *God-Breathed*, we want to journey together to recapture the awe, the mystery, the passion, and the power of God's words in his book. The Bible is no ordinary book. Within its pages are hidden the answers to our every need, direction for our lives, and practical insights for living a life of fulfillment and joy. That is not merely hype; it is what the Author of the book intended from the very beginning.

Consider the following true story about how the consummate master of words unveiled the meaning of Scripture to those he loved.

It had been the worst week of their lives. The two travelers tried to sort things out as they walked the seven miles from the city of Jerusalem to the village of Emmaus. Their greatest hope for being freed from the oppression of the Roman Empire had been in a man they thought was their Messiah. But three days ago he had been taken by the Romans and crucified. Their hopes had died with the death of the one they called Jesus.

That's the way life tends to be. We hope for things, and some things even work out; but, more often than not, we face disappointments, heartache, and loss. Even though we try to find meaning and joy during troubled times, it's an ongoing struggle. That's how these two men may have felt as they walked together along the dusty road.

"I don't know what to think about it," the first one said.

"I don't either," the other replied. "I've heard that Peter himself saw the empty tomb."

"Yeah," his companion countered, "but that doesn't necessarily mean Jesus was raised from the dead like the women are claiming."

About that time, a stranger joined them on their journey. "What are you two talking about?" he asked.

One of the two, whose name was Cleopas, responded, "You must be the only person in Jerusalem who hasn't heard about all the things that have happened there the last few days" (Luke 24:18).

"What things?" the stranger asked.

The two companions told the uninformed stranger all about Jesus—who they had believed he was, how he'd been crucified, and how he was now reported to have risen from the dead. They may have shared their emotional ups and downs. They no doubt talked about the joy they had experienced with Jesus, the hope they had placed in him, and their disappointment in the fact that the Romans had killed him.

After hearing what the two travelers said, and sensing their confusion, the stranger began to quote the words of God to them. Drawing upon the writings of Moses and all the prophets, he explained to them what the Scriptures said and meant about this Messiah whose name was Jesus.

When they arrived at their destination, the two men asked their new friend to join them for a meal and a night's stay. When they sat down to eat, the stranger broke the bread, blessed it, and handed it to them. Then something astonishing happened. The men recognized this stranger as none other than Jesus himself. And then he vanished before their very eyes. They turned to each other in amazement and said, "Didn't our hearts burn within us as he talked with us on the road and explained the Scriptures to us?" (Luke 24:32).

These two companions had heard from childhood the words Jesus quoted to them from the Scriptures. They had grown up reading these Scriptures, but the master of powerful words breathed new life into them. And as he did, he inspired and warmed their hearts, transformed disappointment into hope, and gave them insights for living a life of joy. That is what God's Word is meant to do for us. "For the word of God is alive and powerful" (Hebrews 4:12). It reveals the true heart of a God who loves us and wants us to know him. God's Word has the power to draw us into an intimate relationship with him that will truly transform our lives.

God Is the Master of Reliable Words

As a nineteen-year-old university student, I was intrigued by the ancient writings of Scripture. Though I was a skeptic, as I've mentioned, I sensed a strange power about the words I saw penned on that sixteen-hundred-year-old manuscript. But I didn't trust them to be reliable. In fact, I initially set out to prove that today's Bible is nothing more than a collection of distorted and unreliable records of historical and mythical events. I reasoned that if we couldn't trust that the writings of Scripture had been accurately handed down over the centuries, we would have no basis for the truth claims of the Bible. Simply put, if the Bible is not a reliable document of history, then everything it says about God and the Christian faith is in question.

Have you ever wondered whether the ancient scribes who copied the Scriptures left things out or added things in? Could God have given Moses *twelve* commandments only to have some scribe along the way decide to eliminate two of them? What if, during the copying of the Gospel of John, a hundred years after he wrote it, a scribe left out five chapters? Imagine if overzealous scribes added to or twisted the recorded things Jesus said or did in order to inject their own ideas. How can we be sure that we have a Bible that accurately represents what God inspired people to write on his behalf? Since we have none of the original manuscripts, how can we know that the copies in our possession are reliable and accurate?

Face it, if we can't be confident that Scripture is a reliable book of history, we can't assert that it is the power-filled Word of God. Sure, God may be the master of powerful words, but if his words have not been passed down accurately to us, the power of those words would be lost.

Today, I am convinced beyond a reasonable doubt that Scripture is reliable and its very words are God's own and have real power. As a university student, somewhere in the hidden recesses of my heart I wanted to believe God was real and cared for me. But I had no true basis for believing that, unless the Bible was reliable.

You don't either.

You may sincerely believe in God and that his Word has power. Yet at some point, that faith will be tested. If your faith is rooted in evidence that the Bible is truly reliable, you will have all the assurance necessary to trust that God's Word is absolutely true. I can assure you, there is clear evidence that God has miraculously superintended the transmission and copying of his words to us, so that we can know we have his truth as he intended. You and I can know that God's Word has been handed down to us reliably; and because of that, we can experience his powerful words in our everyday lives. That is what this book is about: knowing with certainty that we can experience the power of God's Word as revealed in the Bible, because it's reliable.

What to Expect

Knowing that the Bible is a reliable conveyor of God's Word is a prerequisite to understanding that his words are powerful. So it would seem logical to discuss the Bible's reliability before dealing with its power. But I want to reverse the order, and here's why: Frankly, I want to appeal to an inner desire that I believe we all share. Somewhere deep inside, you no doubt find the idea appealing that there is an all-powerful being in the universe who loves you dearly. It speaks to a deep desire in every human heart. I want to appeal to that desire before I appeal to your intellect. That's why I want to start by sharing with you how and why God's book has power. My hope is that this groundwork will help you capture more deeply the beauty, mystery, and intrigue of God's Word. To truly sense the power of Scripture is to be captivated by its Author and to develop a true love for him and a longing to know the deep meaning of the words he has recorded for you.

So in the next seven chapters, we will explore the power of Scripture—how it is truly a living book; what its true purpose is; how it was meant to be interpreted; how it is relevant to your everyday life; and how you can gain a true love for this unique, one-of-a-kind document.

After we've been gripped by the power of the God-breathed Word, we will uncover how truly reliable it is, and we will develop a deepened trust that the words in the Bible have been accurately passed down to us. This is what gives us assurance that God has revealed his true nature to us. We will examine how Scripture is reliable using modern tests for any book's reliability; we'll confront apparent contradictions in Scripture; and we'll explain how the Bible can become more alive *to you*.

Warning! Be prepared to be captivated by God's Word. When we truly understand and experience the power and reliability of Scripture, our "hearts will burn within us." This is because we are not simply talking about recorded history and stories of biblical characters. We are talking about a book that is strangely alive.

My prayer is that you will discover in the God-breathed words of Scripture a greater power and relevance to your own life. There is a mystery to God's book, and he wants you to discover it. There are treasures and insights you need in order to deal with the challenges of life. And God wants you to find them by looking for *him* in his Word. " 'If you look for me wholeheartedly, you will find me. I will be found by you,' says the LORD" (Jeremiah 29:13–14).

Let's start looking!

SECTION ONE

✳

The Power
of Scripture

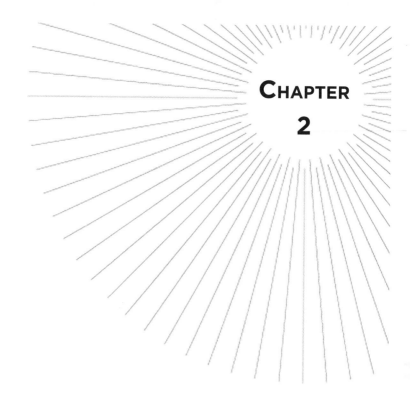

CHAPTER 2

Why the Bible Is Alive

Talk about a tense moment! I was nervous, really nervous. With eyes shut, I prayed that God would allow our ministry to possess what I dearly hoped for—at least one small fragment of an ancient New Testament manuscript. We had just acquired some rare Egyptian burial artifacts, between 1,600 and 2,200 years old, in the hopes that hidden within them we would find fragments of ancient scriptural writings. We had waited for two days while a team of experts carefully dismantled the pieces, and the moment of truth had now arrived.

It was December 6, 2013. Our ministry had organized an unprecedented event in Plano, Texas, that brought together highly specialized scholars in ancient languages, including Coptic and Greek. Coptic was the last stages of the written Egyptian language after the Greeks conquered Egypt. The writings beneath the outer surface of these artifacts would probably be in either Greek or Coptic. I was seated no more than fifteen feet from the table at which these trained specialists had been working for hours. It wasn't the artifacts themselves that interested me; it was their infrastructure, which comprised layers of papyrus (ancient writing paper) dating to between the third century BC and the fifth century AD. These experts had been tediously extracting and identifying the papyri from within the rare Egyptian burial artifacts we had acquired. I was waiting—as patiently as I could—to learn whether what they found would be of a biblical nature.

Dr. Scott Carroll, an ancient manuscript specialist, was ready to announce his findings. He was surrounded by a gallery of about two hundred "invitation only" Christian apologists and leaders who were participating and watching to see what was about to be revealed. The moment of truth was about to arrive.

What Would We Find?

As I sat in nervous anticipation of what Scott and his team were about to disclose, my thoughts went back to how I had gotten to this place.

Scott was the one who had previously arranged my acquisition of a Hebrew Torah, which I named the Lodz Torah.

It was a 540-year-old scroll of the first five books of the Hebrew Bible. I had been displaying it during my speaking engagements. It helped me explain how Scripture was truly reliable in ways I had never dreamed possible. The audience response, especially from young people, was amazing. The teaching value of the Lodz Torah led me to pray that God would allow our ministry to obtain an ancient New Testament manuscript. Displaying such an artifact to thousands of young people and adults would bring them face-to-face with the reality of the written truth about Christ and his life-transforming message. So I naturally thought of Scott Carroll as the person to locate a New Testament manuscript for us.

I had first met Scott two years earlier at a small seminar at Baylor University where he was carefully dismantling papyri from the inside structures of ancient Egyptian mummy coverings (called *cartonnage*). He had developed his own proprietary methods for this extraction process that had led to extraordinary discoveries of ancient classical and biblical texts. The papyri we watched him extract at the Baylor seminar were for the Green Collection, which Scott was directing at the time. He had helped that group amass a collection of more than fifty thousand ancient artifacts, papyri, and parchments valued at millions of dollars. If anyone could locate an ancient New Testament fragment for us, it was Scott Carroll.

I was fascinated by Scott's work. His research and many contacts within the field of ancient and medieval manuscript study gave him a unique understanding of what to look for. Rather than searching for manuscripts at archaeological dig sites, Scott sought to legally obtain ancient cartonnage that had an infrastructure composed largely of discarded papyri.

Papyrus, of course, is the papery substance people wrote on during the time of Christ. Once a papyrus document began to deteriorate or the writing started to fade, it was copied onto a new papyrus and the original was discarded. This was true of the apostles' writings as well. But the ancients did not live in a throwaway society as we do today. Nothing that could be used again or repaired was ever trashed. People often gathered up discarded pieces of papyrus to, in effect, recycle them. They would dampen them and press them together to form various items.

Front of Egyptian mask

The Egyptian burial artifacts I saw Scott dismantling at Baylor were made of pressed layers of papyri. Egyptian mortuary priests used discarded papyri to form papier-mâché, which they used as the infrastructure of mummy coverings or other objects. They sometimes covered the papyrus mold with plaster and painted it with silver or gold. To visualize the process, think of tearing the pages out of a worn book, wetting them down, and then pasting them onto the face of a department store mannequin, shaping the nose, brow, lips, and ears. Then after the paper dries, lacquer and paint the form in flesh colors, and you have a mask. This papier-mâché technique was also used to create various other things besides mummy coverings. It was used to make decorative panels, reinforcements for book covers and bindings, and even household items.

Our ministry commissioned Scott to locate one or more of these reconstituted items in hopes of discovering biblical writings on the papyri from which the papier-mâché was made. Eventually, Scott found for us what he believed to be a good specimen. Rather than rushing to extract the papyrus from these ancient artifacts, we decided to create an experience so that other people could learn from the process as well. We invited over two hundred apologists, Christian leaders, laypeople, and highly specialized scholars in ancient languages to what became the "Discover the Evidence" event.

After lunch on the second day, we all gathered back into the "examination room." Scott and his colleagues had continued to work through lunch to carefully extract the papyri from the cartonnage and had identified a number of pieces. This was the moment I had been waiting for. I could clearly see the many papyri fragments that were laid out all over the table. Language scholars were huddled over them with magnifying glasses.

As the crowd settled in, Scott cleared his voice. "Let me start with Josh's stuff."

I was trying to be calm. My grandson was sitting on my lap. Dottie, my wife, was seated to my right, and one of my colleagues was to my left. With a pair of tweezers, Scott carefully picked up a papyrus fragment and looked toward me. I took a deep breath.

"Here is a paraphrase of the Gospels—a biblical Coptic text— fourth century." My colleague took hold of my arm and said nothing. I simply took another deep breath, looked toward the ceiling, and whispered, "Yes! Thank you, Lord!"

Scott set the fragment down and picked up another. "Here is a second text from the Gospel of Mark, three lines. . .very nice biblical, unsealed, uncial text."

Back of Egyptian mask

He repeated this process again and again. After the initial analysis and identification was made, we found that we were the stewards of six ancient New Testament passages and one Old Testament manuscript fragment—seven treasures in all! While all the manuscripts are yet unpublished and must be further scrutinized to determine the exact content and more precise dating, we do know what passages these are from and the approximate time period. These included a manuscript fragment from Jeremiah 33, which was possibly the earliest known Coptic papyrus of this passage in existence today. There were also manuscripts of Mark 15, John 14, Matthew 6 and 7, and 1 John 2—all possibly the earliest papyrus records of these passages in any language in existence today and Galatians 4, which dates as one of the earliest known papyrus passages ever recorded. These treasures were far beyond my expectations. I was utterly elated!

I walked to the table and gazed at the tan-colored fragments. As I lightly touched them, a wave of emotion swept over me. God had actually answered my prayer. I was humbled that he would allow me to share these treasures with the world. It reminded me of the emotions

I had felt as a nineteen-year-old when I set eyes for the very first time on that ancient biblical manuscript in Glasgow. Again, there seemed to be power in those fragments.

When I visited Scotland as a rebellious teenager, I was far from humble. My arrogance had gotten the better of me. I was out to prove to a group of Christian students that their faith in Christ and the Bible was both foolish and unfounded. When I scoffed at them, they challenged me to examine the evidence that the Bible was reliable and that Christ was who he claimed to be. I accepted that challenge in pride, and my journey began right there in Glasgow.

I made my way from the libraries and museums of Scotland to the English libraries of Cambridge, Oxford, and Manchester. I examined and studied the ancient manuscripts housed there, including the earliest known manuscripts, at the time, of the New Testament. Before my journey was over, I spent months researching at universities in Germany, France, and Switzerland. After devouring dozens of books and speaking with leading scholars, I ended up at the Evangelical Library on Chiltern Street in London. It was about 6:30 in the evening when I pushed the many books aside that were gathered around me. Leaning back in my chair, I stared up at the ceiling and spoke these words aloud without even thinking: "It's true!" I repeated them two more times. "It's true. It really is true!"

A flood of emotions swept over me as I realized that the biblical record of Christ's life, death, and resurrection was recorded accurately and was in fact true. The truth that Christ was God's Son penetrated deep into my soul. I could no longer reject the reality of Christ and be intellectually honest with myself. The impact of that realization was truly a defining moment for me. I now recognized that I was not rejecting Christ for any intellectual reason, but for emotional reasons. I was slowly coming to grips with my rebellion and rejection of Christianity. I began to see that my life of sin was standing between me and a loving God who had sent his Son to die in my place. The power and profound meaning of those ancient manuscripts brought me face-to-face with the person of truth, and his name was Jesus.

Are These Writings Really Alive?

Thinking back, I realized that the bombshell epiphany I had in that London library had been set up earlier by my examinations of the ancient fragments of papyrus in the museums and libraries of Europe. Seeing copied manuscripts of the apostles' letters led me to realize that a real person had copied those texts for an important reason. The writer—or, more accurately, the copier—obviously felt that the message in those letters was so valuable that it must be passed on to the next generation. It was as if the original writings were alive, and each newly copied manuscript preserved and extended that life.

It dawned on me that these handwritten manuscripts had been copied by people who wanted to keep the story of Jesus alive. Behind each ancient manuscript copy of Scripture was a person who had carefully and reverently written down each word, letter for letter. The ink placed on each papyrus seemed to reach out to me and say, "The truth of these words about Jesus Christ has given others new life. They are written for you, too. Will you believe in Christ and experience a new life in him?"

That is the message the apostle John had written on the original papyrus a few centuries before the copies were made. When John realized who Jesus really was, he committed his experiences to writing and explained why he did it: "The disciples saw Jesus do many other miraculous signs in addition to the ones recorded in this book. But these are written so that you may continue to believe that Jesus is the Messiah, the Son of God, and that by believing in him you will have life" (John 20:30–31).

As I looked at and touched the fragment copies of lines that had originally been penned by Mark, John, Matthew, and Paul, I realized these words had an alluring power to them. The people who had copied these letters certainly recognized their power. Remember, these fragments dated back as far as AD 350, which was before they were officially recognized by a church council as the inspired Word of God. So the copiers would not have been aware that what they were copying would eventually be recognized as Scripture. The New Testament wasn't canonized by the church until the councils of Hippo in AD 393 and Carthage in AD 397.

What made the apostle's writings so compelling that people kept copying them for hundreds of years, even before they were officially recognized as Scripture? They obviously felt that the truth of the apostles' letters was relevant to them, but why? Why were these particular writings so captivating and important?

The answer to that question is simple, but no less amazing. God had inspired his apostles to communicate his universal truth in written words, and then kept those words alive through the ever-present person of the Holy Spirit. The Word was alive because the Holy Spirit was speaking his eternal truth directly to his people. The ancient fragment of 1 John 2 that I acquired is a prime example of how God's Word was alive to those in the fourth century and is still alive today.

Just prior to the time when this fragment of 1 John 2 was copied, around AD 320, a Libyan elder in the Alexandria church in Egypt, named Arius, was causing quite a controversy. He advocated that Jesus was a created being and not eternally coexistent with the Father. Christ's deity was freshly under attack within the Egyptian Christian community, and it caused an uproar.

This wasn't the first time Christ's deity had been called into question in the early church. Just over fifty years after Jesus ascended into heaven, a heretical faction of the church began denying the apostles' teachings and claimed that Jesus was not God in the flesh.

The apostle John wrote his first letter to combat these falsehoods. It so happened that the fragment of John that God had allowed me to acquire addressed this very issue.

John warned the church about antichrists—those who claimed Jesus was not the Christ, the true Son of God. The Coptic words on the fragment I have now read: "I am writing to you not because you don't know the truth but because you know the difference between truth and lies" (1 John 2:21). John went on to ask and answer an important question: "And who is a liar? Anyone who says that Jesus is not the Christ. Anyone who denies the Father and the Son is an antichrist" (1 John 2:22). And John then nailed it down and explained why what he was writing was so powerfully true:

> *I am writing these things to warn you about those who want to lead you astray. But you have received the Holy Spirit, and he lives within you, so you don't need anyone to teach you what is true. For the Spirit teaches you everything you need to know, and what he teaches is true—it is not a lie. So just as he has taught you, remain in fellowship with Christ. (1 John 2:26–27)*

The words of John's message were true and powerful because they were the living words of God, who was, and still is today, declaring that Jesus is the Christ. God wanted the people in the first century to believe that important and eternal truth. And he wants us to believe as well. This extraordinary truth is presented in an extraordinary writing that was communicated by the Holy Spirit. These words from God were made alive to the people in the first century, when they were first penned, and in the fourth century, when these surviving fragments were copied, because God's Spirit communicated them. Through the Holy Spirit guiding faithful copyists, he has used those same words to communicate the same truth down through the ages to this very day.

The apostle Paul explains it clearly when he writes: "When we tell you these things [the truth of God], we do not use words that come from human wisdom. Instead we speak words given to us by the Spirit, using the Spirit's words to explain spiritual truths. But people who aren't spiritual can't receive these truths from God's Spirit. It all sounds foolish to them and they can't understand it, for only those who are spiritual can understand what the Spirit means" (1 Corinthians 2:13–14).

The person who copied 1 John 2 around AD 350 no doubt felt the living power of each word. The Egyptian Christians certainly did. They understood these writings were alive through God's Spirit. They wanted to counter the false teachings that Arius was asserting about Christ, and to be certain that their children accepted Jesus as the Son of God who had the power to forgive them and make them his children. The same is true for us today. Those words in 1 John are alive and relevant. There are people within our generation who claim that Jesus was simply a good teacher. They assert he is not the Son of God or our only means of salvation. They say there are many ways to God and that Jesus was merely a man with a good message. But we know that isn't true, because God's Spirit declares in his Word that Jesus is the Christ, and anyone who says otherwise is wrong. God's Word declares the truth, and the Holy Spirit of God confirms it to those with open minds and hearts.

The writer of Hebrews, along with the apostles, claimed that "the word of God is alive" (Hebrews 4:12). That is true because the truth and message of Scripture belong to the living God, who directly explains his spiritual truths to every generation within every culture of the world. There is no other book like the Bible. You may read a novel and be touched deeply by it. You may read a book of poetry or an inspiring Christian book and be profoundly moved. But these kinds of books are not the "word of God." God may certainly use whatever you read to minister to you, but it is his Word and his truth that are uniquely powerful and alive and will remain alive forever. "Heaven and earth will disappear," Jesus said, "but my words will remain forever" (Matthew 24:35).

Think of it: God's words have been alive and powerful—invigorated by the ever-present Holy Spirit—since Moses penned the first five books, the Pentateuch, more than three thousand years ago. They will remain alive through the eons of time. That is what captivated me as I reverently touched the New Testament fragments I had acquired. God's book is a living document that he wants you and me to read. It contains his vocabulary. They are his eternal words. He is there, wanting to speak his living words directly to you and teach you their transforming meaning. But what does he want to teach me? What does he want to teach you?

What the living Word wants to say and teach has eluded many people. The religious leaders in Jesus' time certainly misunderstood the purpose of Scripture. Everything from Genesis to Malachi was written and alive then, but most of the people were not in tune with God's Spirit and therefore did not understand its meaning. The Bible has a clear purpose, and when we understand that purpose, we can truly capture its life-changing truth. Know the true purpose of God's living book and you will taste of its relevance. That is the subject of the next chapter.

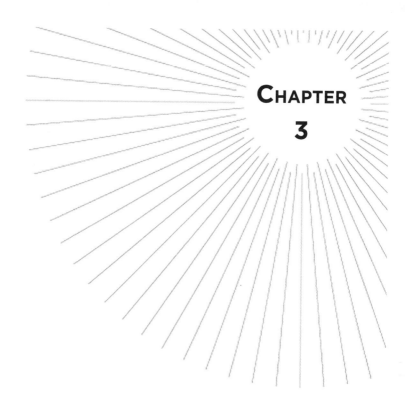

The True Purpose of the Bible

Dottie was practically in tears. She had come home from a meeting at school very hurt by what a student's mother had said about one of our kids. My first inclination was to think of a Scripture passage that would guide my wife's thinking on the situation and then follow it up with an applicable message on the right action she should take.

That is what Scripture is all about, right? Haven't you been taught that the purpose of the Bible is to teach us how to think right and act right? I certainly thought that was the case early in my Christian life.

My natural impulse was to immediately point Dottie to what she should believe about responding to the sharp-tongued person who had criticized our child. Naturally, Dottie wanted to set the person straight. But I could point out that she needed to counter her thinking with a passage such as Deuteronomy 32:34–35: "The LORD says, '. . . I will take revenge; I will pay them back.'" I was certain that Dottie would calm down if she would just get her thinking realigned with God's Word and believe that God was truly the judge in this situation, not her.

Next, Dottie needed to act rightly toward this person. So maybe I could advise her by saying something like: "Well, honey, don't let all this get to you. You need to be patient and kind to this mother, even though she doesn't necessarily deserve it." I was sure that was what God would want Dottie to do. I know that Scripture tells us how to act when people offend us. "Don't retaliate with insults when people insult you [or your kids]. Instead, pay them back with a blessing. That is what God has called you to do, and he will grant you his blessing" (1 Peter 3:9).

Seeing Only Part of the Purpose

There was nothing wrong about the guidance I thought about giving to Dottie. And what better place to find that guidance than Scripture. She, like everyone, needed to think rightly and act rightly. Some people would go so far as to say that God gave us his Word entirely for doctrinal and behavioral purposes to teach us to think and act rightly. They might point to 2 Timothy to assert that correct beliefs and right living are what Scripture is all about: "All Scripture is inspired by God and profitable for teaching, for reproof, for correction" (2 Timothy 3:16 NASB).

Certainly doctrinal and behavioral guidance are part of God's purpose for Scripture. The English word *teaching* in 2 Timothy 3:16 is from the Greek word *didaskalia*, which means "doctrine" or "correct thinking." So Paul is truly explaining that God gave us his Word so that we might believe correctly.

The word *correction* in this passage is from the Greek word *epanorthosis*, which means "restoration to an upright or right state of living" or "improvement in character." So Paul is certainly telling Timothy, and us, that the Bible is God's way of correcting us when we're wrong and restoring us to right living. Therefore, we have the Bible to teach us how to believe rightly and live rightly.

Though this guidance is an important aspect of Scripture, it is not the full picture. In fact, if we fail to place in the proper context the Bible's teaching about thinking rightly and living rightly, we may miss the true purpose of Scripture. That was one of the reasons the religious leaders of Jesus' day were so far off; they elevated "right belief" and "right living" out of their proper context.

The Pharisees and Sadducees were scholars in religious law, and they were taken aback by Jesus, this upstart young rabbi who was challenging them. Jesus was gathering quite a following and seemed to be upstaging them. So they tried repeatedly to trip him up, in hopes of making him look bad in front of the crowds.

The Sadducees in particular didn't believe in the doctrine of the resurrection. So they posed a tricky theological question in hopes of confusing the master teacher. But he shot back a clear answer that pointed to Scripture as our guide to what to believe. "Haven't you ever read about this in the Scriptures? Long after Abraham, Isaac, and Jacob had died, God said, 'I am the God of Abraham, the God of Isaac, and the God of Jacob.' So he is the God of the living, not the dead" (Matthew 22:31–32).

Jesus quoted from Exodus 3:6 to inform us about the resurrection of the dead. Jesus later said, "I am the resurrection and the life. Those who believe in me even though they die like everyone else, will live again" (John 11:25). Here the value of the Bible as a guide to right beliefs is unambiguously affirmed. The Old Testament teachings, Jesus' words, and the writings of the apostles are our authority for determining right doctrine. They are there to instruct us in how to believe and think rightly.

The religious leaders of Jesus' day were big on doctrine. If you didn't believe correctly, they nailed you. They insisted on absolute conformity in every detail to the letter of the law. They saw Scripture as a checklist of dos and don'ts. On one particular day, they set out to trap Jesus with a tax question. They asked, "Is it right to pay taxes to Caesar or not?" Jesus responded, "'Here, show me the coin used for the tax.' When they handed him a Roman coin, he asked, 'Whose picture and title are stamped on it?' 'Caesar's,' they replied. 'Well, then,' he said, 'give to Caesar what belongs to Caesar, and give to God what belongs to God' " (Matthew 22:17, 19–21).

Of course, the Pharisees were asking a politically charged question to trap Jesus. But he simply pointed out that we are to give obedience to whom obedience is due. Jesus upheld the commands of Scripture and repeatedly told us we are to follow the laws, teachings, and instructions of Scripture. In other words, the Bible has a behavioral purpose. We are instructed to do this, avoid that, embrace these thoughts, and abstain from those actions. It is an instruction book on how to live rightly.

The doctrines and commands of Scripture act as two guardrails to guide us down the right path in life. The teachings of Scripture (doctrine) keep us thinking and believing rightly. The instructions of Scripture (commands) keep us acting and living rightly. But without the proper context, we can miss the true purpose of Scripture, which is to guide us into keeping right thinking and right living *in balance*. We can easily overemphasize the importance of the law and focus on knowing all the right doctrines. This can lead to arrogance and the acquisition of knowledge for the mere sake of having it. We can overemphasize adherence to the law, and this can lead to legalistic behavior and judgmental attitudes. Such legalism is what characterized the Pharisees. Their believing and living were out of balance because they failed to understand the most important command of all.

My friend David Ferguson of Intimate Life Ministries of Austin, Texas, has written extensively on what he calls "The Forgotten Purpose of Scripture." David has impacted my life and thinking regarding Christ and the Scriptures. The following section is drawn from his insights on God's relational intent of his Word.

Understanding the Relational Purpose of the Bible

Jesus explained the true purpose of Scripture when he answered a question posed to him by an expert in religious law: "'Which is the most important commandment in the law of Moses?' Jesus replied, 'You must love the LORD your God with all your heart, all your soul, and all your mind.' This is the first and greatest commandment. A second is equally important: 'Love your neighbor as yourself'" (Matthew 22:36–39).

Jesus first quotes from Deuteronomy 6:5, which was part of the *Shema*, a liturgical prayer recited by the religious leaders at the beginning and close of every day: "The LORD is our God, the LORD is one!" (Deuteronomy 6:4 NASB). Then he combines the command-ment to love God found in Deuteronomy 6 with a command from Leviticus 19:18 to love your neighbor as yourself.

Jesus told this inquiring Pharisee that the greatest, most important commandments are to love God with everything we have and to love our neighbors as we love ourselves. But Jesus didn't stop there. He followed up with a most profound statement: "The entire law and all the demands of the prophets are based on these two command-ments" (Matthew 22:40). In other words, all right teaching and all right living hang on the commandments to love God and love one another. Jesus told this religious expert—and all of us—that Scripture was given to lead us into a deeper love relationship with the One who wrote the book, and then also with everyone around us.

The Pharisees and other religious leaders seemingly grasped the doctrinal and behavioral purposes of Scripture. What they failed to understand was the connection between right beliefs, right behavior, and right relationships. From what I've observed, many people in our day fail to see that connection as well.

What Jesus said was extremely important, but it wasn't new. The Hebrew Scriptures are filled with connections between truth (beliefs and commands) and relationships. As King David writes in one of his psalms, "I am always aware of your unfailing love, and I have lived according to your truth" (Psalm 26:3). Then he prays, "Teach me your ways, O LORD, that I may live according to your truth!" (Psalm 86:11). The Old Testament writers understood *truth* within the context of *relationships*. Jesus' declaration simply reframed doctrinal beliefs and obedience, restoring them to their rightful place within the context of relationship, a perspective that had been lost by the religious leaders of his day. He proclaimed that there was a *relational purpose* for God's Word.

What Jesus did when he answered the Pharisees' question is

important to us today because it establishes the proper context for reading and understanding the Bible. Rather than viewing Scripture as a book that merely teaches us how to believe and how to act, Jesus shows us that everything is rooted in how we ought to *love*. By distilling all the doctrinal and behavioral truths of the Bible down to a simple two-part statement—*love God and love each other*—the Lord of the universe showed us that the dual boundaries of *what we believe* and *how we behave* are intended to be understood and experienced within the framework of deep, loving relationships with him and with one another.[1]

The Bible reveals a personal God, who would "speak to Moses face to face, as one speaks to a friend" (Exodus 33:11). It reveals "a God who is passionate about his relationship with you" (Exodus 34:14). From the first word Moses penned in the book of Genesis to the last word John wrote in Revelation, Scripture reflects the loving heart of a God who wants us to know him intimately so we can enjoy all the benefits of our relationship with him.

Moses understood this, of course. He begged God, "If you are pleased with me, teach me your ways *so I may know you*" (Exodus 33:13 NIV, emphasis added). Jesus, in praying to his Father, taught his disciples an important truth: "This is the way to have eternal life—to know you, the only true God, and Jesus Christ, the one you sent to earth" (John 17:3). God spoke through Hosea the prophet, who said, "Oh, that we might know the LORD! Let us press on to know him. . . . I want you to show love, not offer sacrifices. I want you to know me" (Hosea 6:3, 6).

It moves me deeply to know that the mighty God of the universe is so relational that he makes himself vulnerable enough to say, "I want you to know me." You might question this astounding fact and say, "It's hard to believe that the infinite and all-sufficient God, who is not limited by time, space, humanity, or anything else, would desire that we know him deeply." But that's how it is: The infinite God is *personal*. And because he is personal, we can love him, worship him, and please him with our trust and obedience. Because he is personal, he can love us, rejoice with us, comfort us, and reveal himself and his ways to us.

God is not a harsh taskmaster who simply wants obedience. His instructions in his Word for thinking and acting rightly are for our benefit. He knows that when we live according to his ways, it brings us joy, fulfillment, and meaning in life.

God's laws and instructions act as boundaries to tell us what is right and wrong. Living within these boundaries is not restrictive; it is protective, and thus in our best interest. As Moses told the nation of Israel, "Obey the LORD's commands and decrees that I am giving you today for your own good" (Deuteronomy 10:13). Obeying God's Word is always in our long-term best interest. It directs us along the best path of living. Wise Solomon said that it is God who "guards the paths of the just and protects those who are faithful to him. Then you will understand what is right, just, and fair, and you will find the right way to go" (Proverbs 2:8–9).

When we fail to allow God's Word to correct us, we most likely suffer the consequences of wrong living. Solomon writes, "Wise choices will watch over you. Understanding will keep you safe" (Proverbs 2:11). But what about people who choose not to follow the truth of wisdom? Solomon addresses them as well: "They rejected my advice and paid no attention when I corrected them. Therefore, they must eat the bitter fruit of living their own way, choking on their own schemes" (Proverbs 1:30–31). But even God's discipline has a relational purpose. The pain we feel when we go our own way is designed to bring us back to God. He wants us back under his umbrella of protection and provision, because ultimately he wants us to experience a life of joy. "I have told you this," Jesus said, "so that my joy may be in you and that your joy may be complete" (John 15:11 NIV).

The Bible: It's All about Relationship

The Bible reveals an infinite God who is holy, all-powerful, and all-knowing—and yet relational. He longs to interact with each one of us. That is the nature of relationship; it is all about wanting to connect intimately with another—and to *know* that person. It is as if God says, "I want you to open up to me and invite me into your life so I can experience every aspect of your life with you. And though I am omniscient, and therefore know all there is to know about you, I want you to reveal yourself fully to me. In turn, I will reveal myself to you, step by step. I want you to know me for who I am." As hard as it may be to comprehend, our infinite, relational God has given us his Holy Spirit and the Bible so we can learn and love and live in an intimate relationship with him.

God offers to give of himself to us, and he longs for us to give ourselves wholly to him as children give themselves to a loving father. Let's consider again what Paul wrote to Timothy about the purpose of Scripture: "All Scripture is inspired by God and profitable for teaching, for reproof, for correction, for training in righteousness" (2 Timothy 3:16 NASB). Scripture is not only profitable for teaching (right thinking) and for reproof and correction (right acting); it is also profitable for our relationships, that is, "for training in righteousness."

The word *training* is translated from the Greek word *paideia*—"to bring up," as in to rear or parent a child. This passage suggests that God's Word is designed to *parent* us.

But how? How can a set of words in a book parent us? Isn't parenting a person-to-person interaction? Jesus explains how the Word of God can be like a parent to us: "I will ask the Father, and he will give you another Advocate, who will never leave you. He is the Holy Spirit, who leads into all truth" (John 14:16–17). God the Father sent his Holy Spirit to *lead* us, or *parent* us. The Bible is alive because the Holy Spirit comes to show us God himself, and his truth, in the words he has written. He helps us understand who God wants us to be and how he wants us to love and live.

You may wonder why we need the parenting of the Holy Spirit if Scripture is all we need for right living and belief. But think of it this way: What is it that really *parents* our children? Is it the directives, instructions, and commands we give them? Those are *behavioral guidelines*, but they are not what raises our kids. It is not "parenting," as a concept, that brings up children; it is the *parents* themselves—relational human beings—who do the work and perform that role. That is the way God designed it. He wants kids to be brought up in loving relationships. Without *relationship* with another person, all attempts to instill right beliefs and right behavior will be ineffective, because they are detached from the necessary elements of personal love and care. As I have often said, truth without relationship leads to rejection; and discipline or correction without relationship leads to anger and resentment. But when we place truth within the context of a loving relationship, we almost always get a positive response.

The Holy Spirit administers Scripture to us like a loving parent, in order to provide us with wisdom through its lessons (Proverbs 3:5), security through its boundaries (Exodus 20), caution through its warnings (Ephesians 4:17–22), and reproof through its discipline (Philippians 2:3–4). We may study God's Word for correct beliefs. We may even obey God's Word for right behavior. But we must not forget *why*. The relational God of the Bible wants us to *experience* his love and the love of those around us. God gave us the Bible because he wants an intimate loving relationship with us, wants us to enjoy intimate loving relationships with others, and wants our relationships together to extend into eternity.

The relational purpose of Scripture is a powerful reality—the amazing truth that God wants *you* to be in an intimate relationship with *him*. Take a moment to allow that truth to sink in. Think of Jesus, through his Holy Spirit, speaking directly to you in very intimate terms. He longs for you to know him intimately. He longs to fulfill you, complete you, and give you joy as you love him and love other people. That is why he has given you his Spirit and his Word. Read what he says to you and me:

> *"You search the Scriptures because you think they give you eternal life. But the Scriptures point to me!" (John 5:39)*

> *"My purpose is to give. . .a rich and satisfying life."* *(John 10:10)*

> *"I have told you this so that my joy may be in you and that your joy may be complete. My command is this: Love each other as I have loved you." (John 15:11–12 NIV)*

> *"I pray that they will all be one, just as you and I are one—as you are in me, Father, and I am in you. And may they be in us so that the world will believe you sent me."* *(John 17:21)*

These words of Jesus have prompted me to think of Scripture in an altogether different way. They have changed the way I see doctrinal truth and have given me a new reason to obey biblical commands. As a young Christian, I read and studied the Bible. At first, I did it to understand what I should believe and how I should live. But over time, those who discipled me helped me to see the *why* behind my believing and behaving. As I began to see God's heart—his motives, his plans, and his purpose for my life—it changed everything. My personal relationships changed. I learned how to take relationships to a deeper level. My sense of purpose and meaning in the world came into focus. I reordered my priorities. Life became an adventure. I embraced a whole new set of plans and goals in life that were exciting and fulfilling—all because I grasped the true purpose of God's Word.

The reordering of my priorities, especially with my wife and children, have been profound due to understanding the relational purpose of God's word. Again, David Ferguson's books and personal teachings have aided me greatly in that journey.[2]

Let me take you back to what I did and what I said to Dottie that day when she was hurt by the insensitive parent of another child. It is true that my wife needed to *think* and *act* rightly. And there were plenty of Scriptures available to guide her. But at that particular moment, she needed to *experience* God's Word within the context of a loving relationship with God and with me, her husband.

Because Dottie was hurting, I knew that she needed to experience "the God of all comfort, who comforts us in all our troubles" (2 Corinthians 1:3–4 NIV). At that moment, Dottie didn't need to hear a passage of Scripture about how God is a just judge or how she needed to be patient and kind toward a person who had been unkind to her. What she needed was for her husband to experience *with her* the second half of Romans 12:15: "Weep with those who weep."

So instead of spouting Scripture, I simply put my arms around her and said, "Honey, I am so sorry that you had to hear those words, and I hurt for you."

That was it—no theology, no "do this" or "do that." No plan for dealing with the wrong, but just a heartfelt expression that relationally identified with her pain. It was that simple. Profoundly simple. Dottie felt *understood* and was *comforted*, and that was all she needed at the moment. A few days later, she came back to me and asked what I thought she could do to address the critical comments about our child. That was then the time for *thinking right* and *acting right* according to Scripture. But relationship—*love*—came first.

Over the years, God has led me on a journey not only to study and apply scriptural truth to my life, but also to love God more intimately and to love those around me more deeply by experiencing God's truth together. Dottie felt loved that day when I experienced a simple but profound truth with her from God's book. I also felt a deeper sense of love and meaning from "the God of all comfort," who smiled upon his children as they relationally experienced the truth of his Word.

I have been greatly motivated to become a student of God's Word. I have wanted to know what it says and what it means. People have told me that the Bible's meaning is often unclear and that it can be interpreted in 101 ways. That's simply not true. You can count on it: there is a relational meaning in every passage of Scripture, and you can understand how it relates to you when you "know the code," so to speak, that unlocks its meaning. When you understand this "code of interpretation," Scripture comes alive. There is a way to interpret Scripture correctly. In the next chapter, I want to help you crack that code of interpretation.

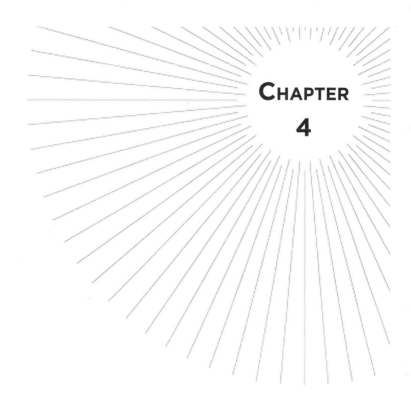

101 Ways to Interpret the Bible? Not Really

Imagine sitting in a Bible study group. Your group leader, Mark, has just finished reading a verse from the book of Galatians: "Bear one another's burdens, and thereby fulfill the law of Christ" (Galatians 6:2 NASB). He looks up from his Bible and scans the faces of the people gathered together. He focuses on Cindy, who is sitting next to you, and asks, "What does this verse mean?"

Cindy, a professing Christian, pauses to reflect on the passage. "Well," she begins, "what this verse means to me is that if someone has a problem, I'm supposed to help him." Mark nods and says, "That's good."

Chad, sitting across the room from Cindy, speaks up. "Hey, Cindy, I've got a little financial problem. I need $2,500 more to buy me a new motorcycle. Can you help carry my burden with, say, a thousand bucks?" The group laughs.

"Seriously, that's actually a good question," Mark says, chuckling. "Are we supposed to help each other out with a financial need like that?"

Then Mark looks directly at *you*. "What does this verse mean to you? Are we supposed to help Chad with his motorcycle purchase?"

Aside from the question about how Christians are to carry each other's burdens, chances are you may not have picked up on the subtle shift in meaning between Mark's first question and Cindy's response. Mark asked, "What does this verse mean?" and Cindy responded, "What this verse means *to me* is. . ."

The question of what Scripture "means to me" or "means to you" is a major point of focus among a lot of people today. Yet it is based on a serious but common error in our approach to interpreting Scripture. Rather than looking to the biblical text to understand *God's* intended meaning of the truth, too many people look for *their own* meaning of the truth. Consequently, they misinterpret passage after passage of Scripture.

There are two basic mistakes people often make when they try to interpret the meaning of the Bible:

1. They inject their own views or emotions into Scripture.
2. They take a verse, word, or passage out of context.

When either of these errors occurs, we misinterpret the true meaning and message of God's truth.

Was the Bible Written to Us?

Let's face it, the Bible isn't always easy to understand. It is composed of sixty-six books and divided into two sections—Old and New Testaments—that were written between two thousand and three thousand years ago by multiple authors, and in three different languages: Hebrew, Aramaic, and Greek. The Scriptures came out of times and cultures vastly different from ours. So it is understandable that many people find the Bible a bit confusing and struggle with interpreting it.

However, it is very important to understand that each book of the Bible has an intended meaning. God wants us to discover that meaning. He wants to reveal himself and his truth within the text so that we might experience him—know and love him, live in his ways, and love those around us as he loves us. Essentially, our task is to interpret the words in order to understand their intended meaning.

But as much as we want to interpret what Scripture means in our own lives, we must remember that nothing in the Bible was spoken or written directly to us who live in the twenty-first century.

Jesus spoke to his disciples, the crowds, and various individuals who lived in the nation of Israel in the first century. Each writer of the books of the New Testament had a certain audience in mind. It's unlikely that these writers foresaw that, some two thousand years later, their writings would be published as the authoritative Holy Bible for the entire human race.

But even though these men wrote within a specific historical context to audiences considerably different from those in the world today; and even though the words of Scripture may not have been written specifically *to* us in the twenty-first century, it doesn't mean they weren't written *for* us. The authors of Scripture wrote *to* a specific audience, yet the truth of those writings is nonetheless *for us* today.

To understand God's truth and how it applies to our lives, we must take two basic steps. First, we must understand the truth that God intended for a specific audience within a specific time in history. Second, we must determine what universal truth God is revealing to us right now. The truth of God's Word transcends history, culture, customs, languages, and timelines. So when we attempt to understand what God wanted the people to know who first received his Word, we also want to understand what he wants us to know today in our own lives.

Remember, God's Word is a *living* document. We can know these things, Paul writes, referring to "the mystery of God," because "it was to us that God revealed these things by his Spirit. For his Spirit searches out everything and shows us God's deep secrets" (1 Corinthians 2:7, 10).

Paul says that he spoke with words given to him by the Spirit "using the Spirit's words to explain spiritual truths" (1 Corinthians 2:13). There are truths from the Old and New Testaments that the Holy Spirit wants to apply to our lives. In order to understand the meaning of these truths, our response should be, "God, what do you intend for me to understand from the passages I read and hear from your book? My heart is open. Help me to discover your intended message to me within the context of our loving relationship."

Interpreting God's Word in this way is a fascinating journey, an exciting process of discovery that not only unlocks the truth that God revealed to his people thousands of years ago, but also uncovers what he wants to reveal to you, in your own life, today.

Cracking the Code of Interpretation

Cracking the code of biblical interpretation involves a process. In order to be accurate, we must draw out the true meaning of what was written or spoken in a given passage. Our task is not to *create* the meaning; it is simply to *uncover* the original intended meaning. The apostle Peter tells us that "no prophecy of Scripture is a matter of one's own interpretation" (2 Peter 1:20 NASB). So instead of *reading into* a text a meaning we think might be there, we must *draw out* the meaning that God intends for us to understand. This process is called *exegesis*.

Exegesis is from the Greek word *exegeomai*, which means "to make known, to unfold in teaching, to declare by making known." This word is used in the Gospel of John when the apostle says that Jesus "has *revealed* God to us" (John 1:18, emphasis added). The New American Standard Bible translates *exegeomai* as "He has *explained* Him" (John 1:18 NASB, emphasis added).

To properly *reveal* and *explain* the meaning of a passage of Scripture, we engage in the process of exegesis by approaching each passage with the probing questions of a news reporter: who? what? where? when? why? and how? Here's the basic process:

1. We examine the text to understand its grammatical construction.
2. We seek to understand the meaning of individual words—literally, figuratively, culturally, etc.
3. We discover the historical context, such as the identity of the author, cultural setting, time frame, etc.

4. We examine the message within the context of paragraphs, chapters, individual books, and the entire scope of scriptural truth.

5. We understand the timeless truth applied to those it was written to at the time.

6. We understand how that timeless truth applies to us today.

As we deliberately follow this process, we crack the code of interpretation. But we must follow it *carefully*. The apostle Paul tells us to "be diligent. . .[in] accurately handling the word of truth" (2 Timothy 2:15 NASB). At first glance, this may seem a daunting challenge; but it won't be if we follow a proven process of determining the meaning of the Bible. There are many valuable study and reference tools to aid us in the process (and we will mention some of these later); but for now, let's look at two key elements involved in the interpretation process: the *determination of meaning* and the *importance of context*.

The Determination of Meaning

Language is composed of words, of course. Words are the building blocks of ideas. And when we assemble words together in sentences and paragraphs, they become the basic unit of communication. This is true of any literary work, and the Bible is a literary work of words, sentences, and paragraphs that communicate God's truth.

But how we interpret these building blocks of verbal communication is important, because their meaning can vary according to the writer's intent. Writers communicate their intent in specific ways that we can analyze and understand to determine meaning. In this section, we will consider two elements that contribute to the determination of meaning: *metaphor* and *grammar*.

Metaphor. A metaphor is a word or phrase that is not meant to be taken literally. Metaphors use a commonly understood word or phrase to suggest its resemblance to something else. The metaphoric word or phrase becomes an illustration that adds impact or clarification to the idea the writer or speaker wants to communicate.

The Bible often uses metaphor for this purpose. Take, for example, Jesus' statement in John 6:35: "I am the bread of life. Whoever comes to me will never be hungry again." What did Jesus mean when he said he was the "bread of life"? Did he mean he was a baked loaf of ground grain mixed with water and yeast? No rational person using ordinary common sense would think that. Common sense tells us that the phrase "bread of life" is not meant to be taken literally; it is a metaphor. In referring to himself as the bread of life, Jesus means that he provides sustenance for our spiritual life, just as a loaf of bread provides sustenance for our physical life. This example is too obvious to question, of course. But it is shocking to hear the contrived interpretations that result when people try to read biblical metaphors literally. A major part of accurate interpretation is merely the application of common sense.

Though the Bible is God's communication of his truth to us, we must keep in mind that it is in the form of a work of literature (and must be, in order to communicate effectively). This means that the same linguistic principles apply to the Bible as to other writings. We can understand passages better if we allow the language to speak in ordinary ways, as it does in all works of literature, instead of imposing a special, artificial standard for language usage in the Bible. This means we cannot take every word of the Bible as *literal*. We must allow its metaphors, similes, and analogies to be what they are, and not force them to be anything other than metaphors, similes, and analogies.

Grammar. In interpreting a passage of Scripture, we must be attentive not only to metaphors, but also to grammar. Grammar involves such things as verb tenses, modifiers, subjects, predicates, and objects. These elements are structural components of sentences and paragraphs, and they are important factors in determining exactly what a written passage means.

For example, verb tense affects the interpretation of Jesus' statement, "I am the bread of life." Determining the tense of the verb—past, present, or future—is a primary factor in understanding its meaning. So what tense did Jesus use in referring to himself as the bread of life?

Jesus did not use the past tense, "I *was* the bread of life"; nor did he use the future tense, "I *will be* the bread of life." Jesus used the present tense: "I *am* the bread of life." The use of the present tense *I am* indicates the unchanging, always-the-same, eternal nature of Christ.

Seeing how Jesus used this same term, in the same tense, in another passage, emphasizes the high importance of grammar to our understanding of Scripture. In John 8:58 Jesus says, "I tell you the truth, before Abraham was even born, I AM!"

At first glance, it might seem to a novice reader that Jesus used terrible grammar by employing conflicting verb tenses within a single sentence. It seems he should have said, "Before Abraham was even born, I *was* [already in existence]." But his use of the present tense in this context, as jarring as it may sound to our ears, conveys accurate information in a way that the past tense would have missed.

Allow me to explain.

In the book of Exodus, when Moses encounters God in the burning bush and God commissions him to persuade Pharaoh to let the people of Israel leave the land of Egypt, Moses asks God how he should respond when the people of Israel ask who sent him. God gives Moses an interesting answer. He says, "Say this to the people of Israel: I AM has sent me to you" (Exodus 3:14). When Jesus used the same term, "I AM," and applied it to himself, his intended meaning was not lost on those who heard him. Because the term "I AM" had special significance to the people as a name that God had given himself, when Jesus applied the same term to himself—in the same present tense—they understood clearly that he was claiming to be one with the eternal God. Entrenched in disbelief, they were outraged at the claim, and it became one of their primary accusations against Jesus.

Jesus, however, *is* the great "I AM." He is the God who always is—the one who lives always in the present tense—the eternal sustainer of the universe and the eternal sustainer of our lives. When we properly understand the grammar and figurative language of Scripture, as with any piece of writing, it helps reveal to us the true meaning of what we read—in this case, the eternal nature of Jesus and his oneness with God.

The Importance of Context

Imagine that you happen to walk past as I'm talking to three or four of my friends. You overhear me say, "No, I'm leaving Dottie next week and she will be staying in California." You don't stop to inquire further, but step over to one of your friends and say, "Did you hear the latest about Josh and Dottie McDowell?"

"No," your friend replies. "What's going on?"

"I just overheard Josh say he's leaving her next week, and he's going to let her keep their house in California."

Shocked and disappointed, your friend glances over toward me. "I can't believe it. There's another one of those Christian speakers who always emphasizes the importance of relationships and yet can't live up to his own message. It's really a shame!"

In this imagined incident, you would have heard me correctly, because I did say I was leaving my wife next week and that she was going to remain at the house in California. But what you didn't hear was the *context*, which was supplied by the sentences spoken before and after the one you heard. Here is the entire conversation, which provides the context for what you overheard:

"I guess you're excited about the upcoming speaking tour in South America," one of my friends says.

"Yeah," I reply, "I'm really looking forward to it."

"You're leaving later this week, right? Is Dottie going with you?" my friend inquires.

"No, I'm leaving Dottie next week and she will be staying in California." I pause. "I'll be gone for three weeks, and I really hate being away from her for that long, all at one time."

What you heard me say in one isolated sentence was accurate, but the interpretation was wrong because my words were taken out of the context of the entire conversation. The point is, we can miss the true meaning of what is said or written if we don't read a text within its full *context*.

Literary Context

We interpret a passage within its context by understanding the *setting*—what comes immediately *before* and *after*. If we fail to understand a particular passage of Scripture within the *whole* of the narrative, we are in danger of misinterpreting the passage we're studying. What complicates the process is when our own life experiences cloud our perception. Take, for example, the Galatians 6:2 passage we quoted in the illustration at the beginning of this chapter. Was it Cindy's responsibility to help with Chad's purchase of a motorcycle in order to live out the apostle Paul's instruction to "bear one another's burdens"? In my early Christian life, I thought this was the case, primarily because I viewed Paul's instruction through the dysfunctional home life of my past.

I grew up in the home of an alcoholic, and I developed a pattern of behavior that made me into what psychologists call a *rescuer*. Each time I saw my father try to hurt my mom, I would step in and try to prevent it. This became a lifelong psychological and emotional pattern for me. I always tried to rescue hurting, struggling people.

When I became a Christian, I continued this unhealthy behavioral pattern, though I didn't realize it was unhealthy. Each time I saw someone hurting or in need, my rescuing compulsion kicked in. But I didn't know it was a compulsion; I thought it was compassion. I thought I was exhibiting Christlike love. When I read, "Bear one another's burdens, and thereby fulfill the law of Christ" (Galatians 6:2 NASB), I felt emotionally responsible to solve other people's problems by trying to remove whatever burdens they had. So if I met someone like Chad who had a financial "need," I felt compelled to help him out. I thought I was fulfilling "the law of Christ" and acting as Jesus would. In reality, I was doing myself harm, and in most cases doing a disservice to the person I thought I was helping—all because I was seeing God's love through my dysfunctional "rescuing lens."

It took the help of others for me to see this passage clearly. The problem was that I was taking Galatians 6:2 out of its literary context. I learned that the verse doesn't teach that carrying another person's burden means taking responsibility for that person's problem or hurt—and especially not for his *wants*, as in the case of Chad and his desire for a motorcycle. Rather, it means coming alongside people and gently helping them deal with their problems. Carrying the burdens of others doesn't mean *taking responsibility* for their problem; it means *being responsible to them*—to comfort, encourage, and support them in their pain or difficulties.

Yes, Galatians 6:2 tells us that we are to "bear one another's burdens." But even though I was reading this verse through my dysfunctional "rescuing lens," I would have interpreted it correctly if I had read the passage within its literary context, which is provided by the surrounding verses. The accurate way to understand verse 2 is made clear in verse 5 (NASB): "For each one will bear his own load." Before I discuss this verse and explain how it provides context, we need to deal with a couple of word definitions.

Notice that verse 2 uses the word *burden* and verse 5 uses the word *load.* There is an important difference between a burden and a load. The Greek word for "burden" is *baros*, which denotes a heavy weight. Jesus used this word when describing the workers toiling in the vineyard who have "borne the burden [*baros*] and the scorching heat of the day" (Matthew 20:12 NASB). This was a heavy burden to bear.

We all face situations that bear down heavily on us, and God is pleased when others put Galatians 6:2 into action by coming alongside to support us in our difficulty. Consider the image of a man carrying a heavy beam across his shoulders. Then two friends come alongside him, put their shoulders on either side of the beam, and help to lift his load. That is the picture here. When we are burdened down with an injury, an illness, the loss of a job, or the loss of a loved one, we need the care, comfort, encouragement, and support of others. We need others to help us lift our heavy load.

In verse 5, Paul uses a different word for "weight" when he says, "Each one will bear his own load" (Galatians 6:5 NASB). The Greek word translated "load" here is *phortion*, which refers to something with little weight, such as the supply pack that a first-century soldier would carry into the field. A more accurate rendering of verse 5 is found in the New Living Translation: "We are each responsible for our own conduct" (Galatians 6:5). It's the same idea Paul conveys in Romans 14:12, when he writes, "Each of us will give a personal account to God."

We all have personal responsibilities, and when we fail in our responsibilities—by using poor judgment or making wrong choices or harboring bad attitudes—we must personally face up to the consequences and not expect another person to do it for us. For someone with a rescuing compulsion to step in and remove the natural and corrective consequences of our irresponsible behavior may rob us of valuable lessons—lessons that may be critical for our continued growth and maturity.

I can't possibly express how valuable this proper interpretation of God's Word has been to me. When I realized that obeying Galatians 6:2 didn't mean I was responsible *for* other people, I was set free to be responsible *to* others—and particularly to those who were hurting. I then began looking for opportunities to allow God's compassionate encouragement, comfort, and support to flow through me to others.

As we have now demonstrated, if we want to draw the correct meaning from a given text, we must see it within its literary context. Why did I misinterpret Galatians 6:2? It wasn't that I misread "bear one another's burdens"; it was that I interpreted the verse outside of its natural context. When I read verse 5 and examined the Greek words for "burden" and "load," understanding that "we are each responsible for our own conduct" allowed me to understand verse 2 within its proper context.

When we read a passage out of context, we're in danger of reading another meaning *into* the text. Scholars call this *eisegesis*, which means "to read into." Most errors of interpretation come from reading into Scripture a meaning that simply isn't there. Much of that can be avoided by reading the text within its literary context.

However, we often need to see more than just a few verses before and after a passage in order to interpret it within its context. We need to see it within the context of the chapter and even the entire Bible. And that is where cross-referencing tools come into play.

Finding Context through Cross-Referencing

Cross-referencing simply means the process of following a topic or a word from one verse to another within the Bible to discover all the book has to say on the subject. The power of cross-referencing comes from the fact that it allows Scripture to interpret Scripture.

Several tools or resources are available to locate cross-references. Many versions of the Bible, especially study Bibles, have cross-references listed in a separate column beside the verses. Your Bible may also have a concordance, which is another cross-referencing aid. Another useful tool is a chain-reference Bible, such as the *Thompson Chain Reference Bible*, the original of its type, which is still available today. A chain-reference Bible has elaborate marginal references and a reference index that makes it easier to trace a given topic throughout the entire Bible.

In our earlier example of the present-tense usage of the term "I AM," we referred to Moses and the burning bush. How did we know that "I AM" was mentioned in Exodus 3:14? The cross-reference margin in our study Bible referred us to the Exodus passage. In fact, in my current study Bible, I find ten cross-references to the words "I AM" listed in the book of John alone. Following that chain of references provides significant context for Jesus' statement "I am the bread of life."

In a simple reading of John 6, we find that it centers entirely on Jesus as our sustainer of life. John's narrative opens with the story of a crowd coming to hear Jesus. After a time, as the people are becoming hungry, Jesus asks his disciple Philip, "Where can we buy bread to feed all these people?" (John 6:5). After Philip replies, "Even if we worked for months, we wouldn't have enough money to feed them!" Jesus performs a miracle by feeding more than five thousand people with five barley loaves and two fish.

"I am the bread of life" is set within the context of this miracle and one other—Jesus walking on water. The way the people responded to these miracles showed that many were following Jesus for the wrong reasons. He said, "I tell you the truth, you want to be with me because I fed you, not because you understood the miraculous signs" (John 6:26).

Jesus met hungry people at the point of their need, but he wanted to do more than address their physical need to eat. "Don't be so concerned about perishable things like food," he said. "Spend your energy seeking the eternal life that the Son of Man can give you. . . . I am the living bread that came down from heaven. Anyone who eats this bread will live forever" (verses 27, 51).

There is so much significance for us in Jesus' statement that he is the bread of life, but we can't interpret that meaning accurately without reading it within the context provided by these other passages. That is how we allow Scripture to interpret itself. The Holy Spirit wants to reveal the truth of his Word to us personally as we understand its relevance to the audience that originally heard it. One way we can do that is by reading the Bible within its own literary context.

Historical Context

The Bible was written in various historical time periods, each of which provides its own context to what was written. The norms of life, communication, and many attitudes and modes of understanding were much different in those times than in ours. The setting, lifestyle, and political structure of those times will affect our understanding of passages written in and to those times. Therefore, in order to explain or reveal the meaning of Scripture, we must see it within the cultural context of its day. Let's consider Jesus' statement "I am the bread of life" in its cultural context. What does the historical setting tell us about how to interpret this verse?

The historical context was the first century during the Roman occupation of Israel. At that time, bread was the main food source. It was not a supplement to the main meal as it is today—something to eat along with our steak, soup, or salad. Bread was the main meal. So Jesus' use of bread as the metaphor for the sustenance of eternal life meant a great deal to his hearers. Just as without bread they would die physically, without Jesus they would die spiritually.

When we read the Bible, we enter into the past—a fifteen-hundred-year span from about 1400 BC to AD 100. Within that time frame there were significant cultural, political, and sociological changes. When we understand the historical setting in which a specific passage was written, we can better understand what God was saying to the original readers and hearers, and why. We can then apply God's universal truth to our lives in the twenty-first century.

Understanding how to interpret Scripture is the first step in experiencing its relevance to our lives. Next, we want to explore how this old relic, the Bible, is meant to be relevant in our everyday lives.

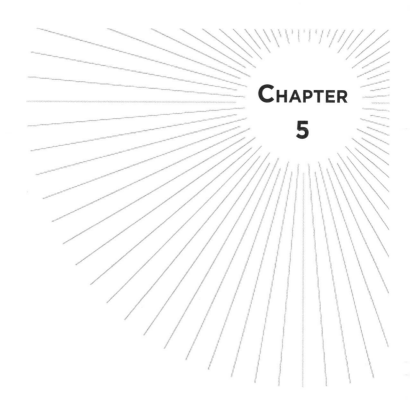

Chapter 5

How the Bible Is Personally Relevant

It was a hectic morning. I had a number of important meetings and I was running late. During breakfast, Dottie had a folder full of agenda items to add to my already filled day. I was trying to deflect them with passive responses like "Okay," "I'll get to that," "Yes, that sounds good," and "All right, I'll try." But Dottie could sense I wasn't really listening and had little intention of getting to her to-do list anytime soon. She bored in and attempted to nail me down.

I lost it. In front of the kids, I started arguing with Dottie. Finally, I exploded. I threw the folder of Dottie's agenda items on the table and said, "I'm out of here." I stormed out the door and drove off.

I wasn't even a mile down the road when I knew I had blown it. Someone like Dr. Phil could probably tell me why I did what I did. A self-help book on anger management could guide me on what to do next. But the Bible? How could an ancient relic like the Bible help with a husband's anger issues? Or, for that matter, how could it help with any marriage, parenting, financial, emotional, or relational issue in life?

As we've already noted, the Bible was written thousands of years ago to cultures completely different from ours. But because its Author is a relational God, and the Holy Spirit is alive and active today to reveal God's truth, Scripture can be applied to every area of our lives. We can be confident of that for three basic reasons: The Bible reveals universal truths that provide an accurate worldview; it addresses how we are meant to live; and it meets us at the point of our need. Let's explore each of these aspects of the Bible one by one.

The Bible Is Relevant to Our Lives Because It Reveals Universal Truths That Provide an Accurate Worldview

We all believe certain things about God, ourselves, others, and all of life. We interpret those things through the lens of our past and present experiences. It is how we see the world—our understanding of reality. This worldview is what we assume to be true about the basic makeup of life and the world around us.

Everyone has a worldview, whether or not we know what it is, because everything we think and do is filtered through our assumptions about how life works. Most people acquire these assumptions from a variety of sources, such as Darwinism, Enlightenment philosophy, Eastern religions, materialism, or postmodernism. Here I want to make a bold statement: None of these philosophies or religions provides a worldview that fits together perfectly and without gaping holes. None of them explains the world we find in our actual experience. In fact, there is only one worldview source that provides complete and satisfying explanations for the world as we experience it: the Bible.

The Old Testament stories of Creation, the Garden of Eden, the Flood, Abraham, the children of Israel, and so on may seem distant and irrelevant today. The life, death, and resurrection of Jesus may at times seem to be isolated incidents that are remembered only on Christmas, Good Friday, and Easter. Yet Scripture is much, much more than just a smattering of isolated stories about the distant past and old rules for human behavior. The Bible tells a story—a huge story, an overarching story, that ultimately ties together and gives meaning to everything in the entire universe and beyond. Within this grand epic, we find a specific story about the human race—how and why we were created, how we went wrong, and God's rescue plan to restore us to his original intent.

It helps us immensely to see this big picture painted so vividly in the Bible. It is then that we are better able to find our place in God's story. The big picture of Scripture can be summarized in the following points:

Creation. The biblical worldview tells us of the origin of all things—time, energy, space, matter, life, and humanity.

Evil. Evil came into our world when an evil being tempted humankind into rejecting God, thus cutting humanity off from the source of eternal life and inflicting pain and death on God's perfect world.

Rescue. God came to earth incarnated as a human being, and he paid the price of death to redeem humanity from the clutches of evil and restore his creation to himself.

New Life. God sent (and continues to send) his Holy Spirit to inhabit humans to trust in Christ, giving us the power to resist sin and live lives in harmony with God.

Restoration. The biblical worldview assures humans of the ultimate restoration of God's original intent, including a perfect world devoid of evil and humans who are sinless and endowed with eternal life.

Seeing this big picture of Scripture gives us a sweeping perspective on what God is doing and how our lives fit into the history of the human race. In other words, it gives us a complete and perfectly dovetailed worldview that unlocks a very specific way of life, a way of knowing what is really true, a picture of what God meant us to be and how we are to live based on our relationship with him.

When we study and read the Bible as a worldview book, we are able to relate the great universal truths of Scripture to our everyday lives. This enables us to understand who we are as humans in relationship to God, what constitutes right from wrong, and how God's way is meant to bring resolution to the physical, relational, social, moral, ethical, economic, and environmental problems of life.

When I stormed out of the house as mad as a hornet that day, my actions were inconsistent with a biblical worldview. Because I was a student of the Word, I knew I had done wrong. As I drove down the road, I said to myself, "McDowell, what in the world is up with you? Get yourself back to the house and clear the slate with your wife." I turned around, went back to the house, apologized to Dottie for blowing up, and asked her to forgive me for hurting her. Later, at dinner, I told the kids I had been wrong for being so disrespectful to their mother that morning, and I asked them to forgive me, too. It gave me an opportunity to let my kids see how Dottie and I resolved our conflict.

What universal truths of Scripture were relevant to me at that moment? Three came to mind that I was intent on following. The first Scripture I quoted to myself was Ephesians 4:26: " 'Don't sin by letting anger control you.' Don't let the sun go down while you are still angry." When I exploded at Dottie, I was guilty of allowing anger to control me. But I wasn't going to be guilty of the second part of that verse. Before the day went by, I was determined to get the slate clean with my wife. And I did.

Two other biblical truths were relevant for me at the time. King Solomon said, "If you ignore criticism, you will end in poverty and disgrace [including relational poverty and disgrace]; if you accept correction, you will be honored" (Proverbs 13:18). He also writes: "A man who refuses to admit his mistakes can never be successful. But if he confesses and forsakes them, he gets another chance" (Proverbs 28:13 TLB).

Following these universal truths of Scripture led me to take responsibility for my negative emotional reaction and resolve the conflict with my wife. God's worldview book has hundreds of such truths and guidance to address every aspect of our lives. God's Word is personally relevant.

The Bible Is Relevant to Our Lives Because It Addresses How We Are Meant to Live

A lot of people see the Bible as a book of dos and don'ts, laws to obey, and instructions to follow. Looking at the Bible in this way misses the point behind its laws, instructions, and commands. Actually, all the guidelines of Scripture are representations of God's ways and how he acts. When we live according to his ways, we experience true joy because we are living the way we were designed to live, as people created in God's image. This was God's intention from the beginning when he said, "Let us make human beings in our image, to be like us. They will reign over. . .all the wild animals on the earth. . . . . So

God created human beings in his own image. In the image of God he created them; male and female he created them" (Genesis 1:26–27).

Scripture teaches us that God is an awesome, eternal being (Isaiah 40:28) who is all-powerful (Psalm 147:5), ever present (Jeremiah 23: 23–24), never changing (Psalm 102:26–27), all-knowing (Isaiah 46:9–10), and perfectly holy (Isaiah 6:3). We humans were created in God's image and likeness, but not in his *infinite* image. Rather, we were created in the image and likeness of God to reflect his capacity to will, reason, love, and create.

Deep within us, God planted these distinguishing characteristics of his own likeness, giving us our capacity to will, reason, create, and form loving relationships. "God is love," John says, "and all who live in love live in God, and God lives in them. And as we live in God, our love grows more perfect" (1 John 4:16–17). God wired us with a longing to live out our relational nature, which includes a longing to love others and a desire for others to love us deeply enough to explore the depths of who we are as people created in God's image.

As relational beings, we were meant to love and be loved. We all want others to discover who we are and to love what they find in us. We want to know others for who they are and love them for being original, one-of-a-kind people. We were created to know others and to be known. We were designed to love and be loved in order to enjoy God and one another. God's book is his instruction manual for how we can maximize our joy in life.

A lot of people get hung up on what they see as the Bible's negativity. In chapter 2 we touched on the reality that God's Word instructs us to avoid some things for our own good. But did you know that every negative command of Scripture derives from two very powerful motivations of God? Every time God says *no*, he does so in order to *provide* for us and *protect* us.

"For I know the plans I have for you," God said to the children of Israel, "plans to prosper you [to provide for you] and not to harm you [to protect you], plans to give you hope and a future" (Jeremiah 29:11 NIV). Each time God gave Israel instructions, it was to provide for and protect his people. He wants to provide for and protect us as well. The motivation of God's heart is *love*, and he wants us to have all that we need to live happy and fulfilled lives. A biblical definition of Godlike love might be stated like this: *Love means making the security, happiness, and welfare of another person as important as our own.* And that is a providing and protecting kind of love.

How Following God's Word Protects Us

More than forty-five years ago, a medical doctor named S. I. McMillen wrote a fascinating book titled *None of These Diseases*. He took more than two dozen commands that God gave to Israel and demonstrated how they were designed to prevent such disorders as dysentery, heart disease, cervical cancer, and arthritis long before the advent of modern medicine. Dr. McMillen writes in his preface:

> *When God led the Israelites out of afflicted Egypt,*
> *he promised them that if they would obey his statutes,*
> *he would put "none of these diseases" upon them. God*
> *guaranteed a freedom from disease that modern medicine*
> *cannot duplicate.*[1]

This, of course, doesn't mean we will never get sick if we always obey God's Word. Yet God's commands act as a protective umbrella against the consequences of wrong choices. Take the instructions regarding our sexual behavior for example. God meant his *no* to be a positive answer for our sex lives.

In biblical terms, sexual immorality is any sexual activity that occurs outside of a marriage between one man and one woman (including extramarital and premarital sex). Scripture states:

You must abstain from. . .sexual immorality. (Acts 15:29)

Run from sexual sin! (1 Corinthians 6:18)

We must not engage in sexual immorality.
(1 Corinthians 10:8)

When we follow the biblical commands to live sexually pure lives and remain faithful to a single marriage partner, our obedience acts as a protective umbrella. We avoid such things as guilt and shame, unplanned pregnancies, sexually transmitted diseases, sexual insecurity, and emotional distress. That kind of protection certainly enhances a couple's sex life within their marriage.

When Dottie and I were first going together, we made a decision early on to wait until marriage before expressing ourselves sexually as a couple. That commitment also meant we would remain sexually faithful to one another after marriage. And we have. Because we both were obedient to God's commands regarding sex, we have been protected from sexually transmitted diseases, feelings of guilt, and the heartache of a pregnancy before marriage. Consequently, we did not experience the heart-wrenching ordeal of giving up a child for adoption or struggling with getting married before we were ready.

We have been protected from the sexual insecurity that can result from being compared to past sexual partners, the emotional distress that premarital sex can bring, and the feelings of betrayal that an extramarital affair can cause.[2]

Following God's relevant instructions on sexual behavior allows a couple to experience the beauty and joy of sex as it was meant to be experienced. The motivation for God's saying no is that he wants the best for us.

We can go down the list of scriptural commands and find all kinds of protection that results from living them out. The Bible tells us not to steal or lie (Exodus 20:15–16). The apostle Paul tells us to "stop telling lies" and to "tell our neighbors the truth" (Ephesians 4:25). Being honest protects us from guilt, shame, a cycle of deceit, and from damaging our relationships with others.

Scripture teaches us to show mercy. Jesus said, "Blessed are the merciful, for they will be shown mercy" (Matthew 5:7 NIV). We get back what we give out; and when we show mercy, we are protected from want, retribution, and unforgiveness (Matthew 5:7; 6:14–15; Luke 6:38).

When we follow God's instructions about being just, showing love and respect toward others, and exercising self-control, we are protected from the many consequences of sin. This doesn't mean that being obedient to God will give us pain-free lives. In fact, Scripture points out that we will sometimes suffer when we do what's right, simply because we live in a world infested with evil. But even such suffering has rewards. In this present life, we will reap spiritual blessings, and in the end God will reward us in eternity.

How Following God's Word Provides for Us

The fact that Dottie and I remained faithful to God's Word before and after we got married has protected us from all the problems I listed above. Being obedient to Scripture in our sexual relationship together has also provided us with many positive blessings. There have been spiritual rewards, such as our consistent relationship with God. We have enjoyed the optimum atmosphere of raising our kids within a married family relationship. Our faithfulness has produced peace of mind and provided trust in the relationship. Rather than the emotional distress that premarital sex can bring, or the feelings of betrayal that follow an extramarital affair, we have enjoyed relational intimacy unobstructed by a breach of trust.

Living lives of honesty provides a clear conscience, gives a sense of accomplishment, builds a reputation of integrity, and develops trusting relationships. Showing mercy provides for blessing, leniency, and forgiveness by others. In every case, when we follow God's way, we reap benefits. The psalmist David makes it clear how beneficial it is to obey God's commands:

> The instructions of the LORD are perfect,
> *reviving the soul.*
> The decrees of the LORD are trustworthy,
> *making wise the simple.*
> The commands of the LORD are right,
> *bringing joy to the heart.*
> The commands of the LORD are clear,
> *giving insight for living.*
> Reverence for the LORD is pure,
> *lasting forever.*
> The laws of the LORD are true,
> *each one is fair.*
> They are more desirable than gold,
> even the finest gold.
> They are sweeter than honey,
> even honey dripping from the comb.
> *They are a warning to your servant,*
> *a great reward for those who obey them.*
> (Psalm 19:7–11, emphasis added)

We were created in God's image and were meant to live according to his ways. When we live in his ways, as dictated in Scripture, we live lives of joy under his loving protection and provision. God's Word is always personally relevant.

The Bible Is Relevant to Our Lives Because God Meets Us at the Point of Our Need

It wasn't as I remembered it. The shingles were half blown off the barn. Some of the windows of the house were broken. Weeds of every kind overgrew the place where I had lived as a kid.

I had taken my four grown children to see what was left of the 120-acre dairy farm I had once called home. I tried to explain to them what the place was like in the early 1940s.

I pointed to the back porch of the dilapidated farmhouse and explained how my older sister made homemade ice cream while I sat and watched her. I told them how my mother could make the best root beer in all of Michigan, and how I'd guzzle all the root beer floats my sister would let me drink.

I then walked my kids toward the precariously leaning corncrib. Pleasant thoughts of homemade ice cream and root beer floats suddenly vanished. We were just a few feet from the old leaning shed when I abruptly stopped. As I stared at the weather-beaten structure, tears began to well up and blur my vision. I felt paralyzed by the memory of a terrible day of shame and abandonment so many years ago.

I was eleven years old at the time. It was a Saturday morning, and I was excited because I was going to watch a small house on our farm being moved to a new location. Workers had jacked up the house and put wheels under it the day before. And so I was anticipating the sight of tractors pulling a house down the road.

My oldest brother, Wilmot, had sued my dad to take possession of the house and half the farm. I was trying to stay out of the family feud and just enjoy the spectacle.

It seemed as if the entire town had turned out for the event. Then, just as the tractors were being attached to the house, my father, drunk as usual, began yelling at Wilmot. The sheriff, who had come to help keep the peace, moved toward my dad to prevent an ugly scene.

But it was too late for that. Most of the townspeople who supported Wilmot began to chant obscenities at my father. Many of my classmates were also there watching all of this. It was more than I could take. I ran down the hill toward the corncrib as fast as I could. Humiliated and ashamed, I climbed into the corncrib and lay there crying as I covered myself with corn.

Hours passed, and no one came looking for me. No one even seemed to notice I was gone, and I felt abandoned and alone. It was a defining moment in my young life. That day solidified my hatred toward my father. I became an angry young man, and that deep resentment haunted me for years to come.

As I stood facing that old shed, the entire scene came back to me with a flood of emotions. The pain resurfaced right there in front of my grown children. They were aware of what had happened, and they sensed what was going on now. By this time, I was openly weeping.

My son and three daughters moved toward me and wrapped their arms around me. They wept with me, stroking my head and shoulders as they spoke words of comfort and encouragement. As I gathered my composure, we found a place to sit. Each of my kids affirmed that I had been a loving father, even though I hadn't had one of my own.

What happened at that moment? My four adult children were faithful to Scripture, and God met me at the point of my need for comfort, encouragement, and affirmation. Because my children were faithful to affirm, comfort, and encourage someone in need, "the Father of compassion and the God of all comfort" (2 Corinthians 1:3 NIV) flowed through them to meet their dad's need of the moment.

We all have certain emotional and relational needs. We have a need for comfort (2 Corinthians 1:3–4), support (Galatians 6:2), care and affirmation (1 Corinthians 12:25), and encouragement (Hebrews 10:24). God is there to meet our needs, and his people are instructed in Scripture to partner with him in meeting needs. These instructions appear at least thirty-five times in the New Testament.

When we are in need of comfort, affirmation, or words of encouragement, as I was, God is there to meet our need and is often pleased to flow his need-meeting power through another person. God is our loving protector and provider, and he is there, directly or indirectly, to meet us at the point of our every need. For additional insights on our biblically based needs and how to meet them see Endnote 3 of this chapter regarding resources from David Ferguson.[3]

God Cares What Happens to You!

Life has a way of wearing on us at times. We can sometimes be tempted to think that God doesn't notice when we are in need of strength, encouragement, or the simple recognition that we are loved. But he is always there. Scripture says, "Give all your worries and cares to God, for he cares about you" (1 Peter 5:7). Because God's Word is reliable, alive, and powerful, we can rely on God to be there for us. He won't let us down.

Recently, God affirmed me in a powerful way that serves as a testimony to the fact that God cares about each and every one of us in very intimate ways. To provide a background for what happened, let me tell you that I have been in ministry, speaking to others about the truth and evidences of the Christian faith, for more than fifty years. Because my primary ministry has been in speaking, a passage in 1 Peter has always been close to me:

> Do you have the gift of speaking? Then speak as though God himself were speaking through you. Do you have the gift of helping others? Do it with all the strength and energy that God supplies. Then everything you do will bring glory to God through Jesus Christ. (1 Peter 4:11)

I now have passed my seventy-fifth year, and it would be natural to wonder whether a person my age can still be relevant in his "golden years." My motto has always been to keep doing what I'm doing "Until the Whole World Hears." I started using that phrase at the close of all my correspondence more than three decades ago. I still do. Though I haven't felt that God wants me to hang it up yet, I must confess I've wondered just how much strength I have left or how long I should keep at it.

Recently, God answered that question through the incident I shared earlier about the fragments of Scripture discovered in the ancient artifacts I had acquired. But I haven't yet told you the backstory, which has to do with how God gave me the affirmation I needed.

My friend Dr. Scott Carroll, who had taken on the task of finding ancient artifacts for our ministry, spent months of research and traveled thousands of miles scouring ancient structures and sites. Finally, he reported back to me.

"Josh, I have looked at more than one hundred artifacts and have found what I believe may be an amazing discovery."

"I'm listening," I replied.

"Well, I can't guarantee it," he continued, "but I found some artifacts that I believe date back to the fourth or fifth century AD. They come from an area that tells me there is a good probability they may have biblical papyri within them."

My heart began to beat faster as Scott related his findings. I swallowed hard and asked, "What's the next step?"

"You give me the go-ahead and I'll make the owner an offer. I think we can get them for the price we discussed."

I told Scott to acquire it all. My mind began to race as he made the arrangements to get the hidden treasures that I felt confident would be used to advance God's kingdom. My hopes were up. My long-awaited dream was about to come true. Or so I thought.

I felt the buzz of the cell phone on my belt. It was a call from Scott. I felt certain he was on a flight back from Europe with the artifacts in hand. Instead, he relayed the bad news that another collector had stepped in and acquired every artifact I had authorized Scott to buy.

Talk about disappointment! I felt my heart sink to my stomach. I felt even worse when I learned later that those artifacts yielded early biblical papyri that were truly valuable and rare. I thought to myself: *Those were supposed to be ours!* I was heartsick. I tried to console myself by saying there were other artifacts out there. But the bitter taste of disappointment lingered.

Weeks passed. Scott kept at it and eventually reported from Europe that he had found another set of ancient artifacts that he felt were worth obtaining. I said, "Let's get it all—right now!"

This time Scott was successful, and we planned the discovery event I described in chapter 2. As each biblical fragment was uncovered at that meeting, I was thrilled. We had in our hands passages from Jeremiah 33; Mark 1; John 14; Matthew 6 and 7; 1 John 2; and Galatians 4. While yet unpublished these were possibly the earliest copies of these passages in existence today—if not the earliest. This of course made them amazingly rare and valuable. But I have to admit that when I compared the seven fragments that we uncovered to the amazing find that had been bought out from under us, a residue of disappointment still lingered.

That is, until I realized what God had actually reserved especially for me.

To my amazement, the seven biblical passages related directly to the message themes I have spoken on my entire ministry life. I have written and spoken about Christ's deity from day one of my ministry. In our 1 John 2 fragment, the apostle is warning believers of those who would lead them astray by claiming that Jesus is not the Son of God. The apostle Paul is doing the same in the Galatians 4 fragment. It was as if God was saying to me, *"Keep speaking this message for me, Josh, until the whole world hears!"*

In my speaking and writing, I have emphasized messianic prophecy, because it gives powerful evidence in support of the major theme of Christ's deity. So I was floored when we discovered that the fifth-century Jeremiah 33 fragment contains the prophecy that a descendent of David's will sit "on the throne of Israel forever." It was as if God was again saying to me, *"Keep speaking this message, Josh, until the whole world hears!"*

Another focus of my ministry has been Christ's resurrection—the ultimate evidence of his deity. Two of the New Testament fragments I now had were from Mark 15 and John 14—both about Christ's death and resurrection. Again I heard God saying, *"Keep speaking this message, Josh, until the whole world hears!"*

Another theme I have emphasized consistently over the years is how God has given believers a way to judge what is true and false and to discern right from wrong. I have spoken and written on this truth extensively, using Matthew 7 to underscore it. Amazingly, God allowed me to obtain the ancient fragment of Matthew 7. It was clear to me that God was saying, *"Keep speaking this message, Josh, until the whole world hears!"*

Finally, there was the fourth-century fragment of Matthew 6 with the words of Jesus telling us to "seek the Kingdom of God above all else, and live righteously, and he [God] will give you everything you need" (Matthew 6:33). God had placed in my hands the very passage that represents the theme of all my relational messages—that when we seek God and his ways morally, ethically, and in all our relationships, he gives us what we need because he is our loving provider and protector. Every one of my six campaigns, spanning more than thirty-five years, has had this core focus. By giving me these seven passage fragments, God made it abundantly clear that he was saying, *"Keep speaking this message, Josh, until the whole world hears!"*

I have no doubt that God permitted us to obtain these ancient living treasures to help young people and old people alike to realize that the Bible is God-inspired and historically reliable. But what really astounds me is that God would ordain that I would be granted seven specific passages that represent what I have been speaking and writing about all my ministry life. Some might say that is a coincidence. I see it as God personally affirming me in what I've been doing for fifty years and urging me to keep going.

My friend who pointed this out to me and helped me connect the dots added this observation: "Josh, do you know what this means? More than sixteen hundred years before you were born, one or more ancient Egyptians formed some cartonnages out of discarded papyri fragments. As they reached into the pile of papyri scraps, their hands picked up seven biblical fragments—fragments that focused on five messages a servant of God would need to have affirmed sixteen centuries later.

"For more than sixteen hundred years," he continued, "those cartonnages stayed hidden from the public. And when you were about to purchase a rare artifact containing a valuable biblical find, what happened? Someone bought it out from under you. Why? It seems clear to me. God wanted you to have a special cartonnage that he had been saving for sixteen centuries just for you! He did this because he loves you and wanted to affirm you in your later years, letting you know that you are still his valuable spokesman and that he would be pleased if you would keep on speaking his message 'until the whole world hears.' "

If this is God's way of saying to me, "Keep it up, my son," then I will respond with a heart of gratitude and humility and say, "Thank you, Lord. I needed assurance and affirmation, and you gave it to me. Again, you met me at my point of need."

As I end this chapter, I want to clarify one thing: Though I am grateful for God's encouragement to continue in his service, I don't for a moment take this as a validation of *my* ministry. This is about *God's* ministry, of which he has so mercifully allowed me to be a part. I couldn't do what I have been doing without God's power and strength. As a young man, I had a lot stacked against me—a home torn apart by alcoholism and anger, the childhood trauma of sexual abuse, my struggles with feelings of inferiority that came out in stuttering speech—yet God took the weak things in my life and made them strong through him.

I am a living example of how God's Word is personally relevant. His Word is relevant to you, too. God inspired men two thousand to three thousand years ago to write words meant to be relevant for you right now in your life's situation. These words are there to tell you that God will never leave you or forsake you. He has comforting words to heal your hurts; a spirit of encouragement for when you are struggling with disappointments; acceptance to say you are loved for who you are, no matter what; security in times of danger to remove your fear of the future; approval that says you are his child; and an everlasting love that says, "Give all your worries and cares to God, for he cares about you" (1 Peter 5:7).

You Were Created for a Unique Purpose

The Bible is personally relevant to you because it affirms your uniqueness and the special way you fit into God's universe. God has created you for a ministry every bit as unique and valuable as mine. It may not be a public ministry; it may not be a full-time or professional ministry. But as Paul says in 1 Corinthians 12, each of us is designed with unique talents that enable us to function as members of his kingdom in ways that no one else can. He compares the church to a body and tells us that each of us is a different and unique part of it. Just as a body must have many different organs and limbs in order to function, we as members of Christ's body also must have unique gifts, talents, and abilities to be used to benefit the whole.

How do you find your unique talent or function? Scripture tells us. In 1 Corinthians 12:4, Paul writes, "There are different kinds of spiritual gifts, but the same Spirit is the source of them all." If you will open yourself to God's Spirit and submit to him, through his leading you will find the place where you are meant to serve.

In whatever way you are called to minister, your ultimate purpose is to bring glory and honor to God by knowing him, being like him, and living according to his ways. As he completes you, your unique meaning in life will come into focus. This unique stamp defines who you are and why you are here.

As part of Christ's body, you have a specific destiny to fulfill: to participate in his mission to reconcile the world by loving God with all your being and loving your neighbor as yourself. And then, in glorious hope and expectation, you will enter into your inheritance of living with God himself in a perfected relationship in a sinless and perfect world for all eternity.

As you can see, the Bible is relevant to every aspect of your life. The pages of Scripture are your road map, and the Holy Spirit is your guide. The Bible may have been written two thousand to three thousand years ago, but its truth is personally relevant today. So I urge you to look to God's Word. It has all you need to understand who you are, your purpose, your destiny, and how you fit into God's universal plan. The Bible is truly relevant today.

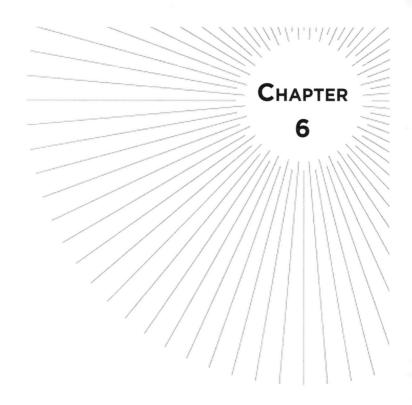

CHAPTER 6

Authored by God or by Man?

The thunder roared. A bolt of lightning flashed from the clouds. The mountain shook violently as flames and smoke shot high into the sky. And then it happened. God spoke. Terrified beings quaking below this spectacular display of natural forces heard with their own ears the same powerful voice that spoke the universe into existence.

This is what happened just over three thousand years ago when God audibly spoke to the children of Israel from Mount Sinai. But he did more that day than make his voice heard. He also presented Moses with "two stone tablets inscribed with the terms of the covenant, written by the finger of God" (Exodus 31:18). God's words were written by God himself.

This was truly a historic and most unusual day. Moses put the event into perspective when he wrote: "Now search all of history, from the time God created people on the earth until now, and search from one end of the heavens to the other. Has anything as great as this ever been seen or heard before?" (Deuteronomy 4:32).

There they were. Two tablets of stone on which God had written his own words for all to see and understand. No one could contend that those words were tainted by any human bias, when God wrote them himself. That was true of the original Ten Commandments, but is it true of the Bible today? Do we have the very words of God spoken and written by God himself? The apostle Paul seems to refer to Scripture this way when he explains that the Jewish people "have been entrusted with the very words of God" (Romans 3:2 NIV). Jesus seems to refer to Scripture this way when he chides the Pharisees, in Matthew 15:6, for misusing the teachings of Scripture: "You cancel the word of God for the sake of your own tradition."

The original tablets of stone would certainly be considered the direct words of God written with no intervening agent. But that was an isolated case. All other Scripture was penned by men such as Moses, King David, the prophets, and the apostles. So if Scripture is God's

Word, what did he do, put these people into some kind of trance in order to take control of their hands and pens to write out his message to us? And if he didn't do that, how can Scripture be considered "the Word of God"?

The True Meaning of Inspiration

Have you ever been inspired while listening to a song or reading a poem? Perhaps you have written an inspiring song or poem yourself. Songs, poems, novels, public speeches, and pep talks from coaches can inspire us. But when we say the Bible is inspired, it means more than having our spirits lifted by a person, song, or book.

The apostle Paul writes that "all Scripture is inspired by God" (2 Timothy 3:16). The word *inspired* is translated from the Greek word *theopneustos*, which literally means "God-breathed" (*theos*, God; *pneō*, to breathe). In other words, God breathed out his words to men, who in turn wrote them down. These men were not God's mindless dictation machines, nor were they placed in a hypnotic state to transmit God's words in writing. Rather, God revealed to their minds what he wanted them to write, and they, as his willing servants, put into writing what he wanted them to say. These men used their own writing skills and talents, but they were very cognizant that the thoughts and words they were writing came directly from God.

The apostle Peter sums it up like this: "No prophecy in Scripture ever came from the prophet's own understanding, or from human initiative. No, those prophets were moved by the Holy Spirit, and they spoke from God" (2 Peter 1:20–21). Peter says that the Holy Spirit superintended God's words so that men wrote what he wanted them to write. Men were God's instruments to convey his message. The apostle Paul makes the same point when he writes, "When we tell you these things, we do not use words that come from human wisdom. Instead, we speak words given to us by the Spirit, using the

Spirit's words to explain spiritual truths" (1 Corinthians 2:13).

God chose numerous ways and means to convey his words through his spokesmen. In the case of Moses, God elected to speak directly to him. "The LORD would speak to Moses face to face, as one speaks to a friend" (Exodus 33:11). Later, Moses told the children of Israel that "the LORD your God will raise up for you a prophet like me. . . . The LORD said to me, '. . .I will put my words in his mouth, and he will tell the people everything I command him'" (Deuteronomy 18:15, 17–18).

Sometimes God communicated to his spokesmen through dreams, as he did with Joseph in Genesis 37. In the case of Isaiah, Ezekiel, Daniel, the apostle John, and others, God spoke to them through visions. At other times, God sent angels to visit his writers (Genesis 19). But most often, the words came through an inner voice of God's Spirit represented in the phrase "according to the word of the Lord." This choice of words is used more than three thousand times throughout Scripture. God wanted us to know him and how we could have a relationship with him, so he carefully communicated "the words of the Lord" through his human spokesmen. The apostle Paul wanted his readers to realize that he was only God's spokesman and not the originator of the message when he said, "I want you to understand that the gospel message I preach is not based on mere human reasoning. I received my message from no human source, and no one taught me. Instead, I received it by direct revelation from Jesus Christ" (Galatians 1:11–12).

Practically every person through whom God chose to inscribe his message made it clear that God was the source of that message. That's why we say that God is the author of Scripture and men were his writers. It was God's spiritual truths conveyed through men to the written page. So when we read the writings of Moses, David, Solomon, Isaiah, Jeremiah, Matthew, Mark, Luke, John, Peter, Paul, and all the other spokesmen of God, we can be assured that we are reading God's words.

Why So Many Writers?

Because God is all-knowing and all-powerful, he could have spoken through one person to convey his universal truth to the human race. But he didn't. He chose to have his truth conveyed across more than forty generations by more than forty different writers from every walk of life. Those men included statesmen, scholars, shepherds, soldiers, poets, prophets, a physician, monarchs, masters, servants, tentmakers, tax collectors, and fishermen. They wrote in a variety of places: in a palace, in a prison, in the wilderness, in a dungeon, on a hillside, and on an island in exile. God chose men of various backgrounds with different talents and different levels of educational training. Their life experiences were just as diverse. They had different personalities, different styles of writing, and different perspectives on life. Each writer brought his own unique human experience to the table, so to speak. And it's clear that this was God's intention.

As humans, we each are shaped and molded by our life experiences. The houses we grew up in, the schools we attended, the parents we had, and the friends we made are all part of the backdrop and cast on the stage of our lives. What happened under these influences, and how we responded to each day's events, greatly shaped who we are today. And because we're each a one-of-a-kind creation of God's, with our own set of life experiences, we each see life in a slightly different way than everyone else. So, if God chose to convey certain truths through you, he most likely would match that message up with your particular personality, gifting, training, and life experiences. This is precisely what God did in selecting his human spokesmen—he spoke through men who would relate humanly to the message he wanted to convey.

Notice that God chose King David to write his message to us about failings, sin, suffering, loss, repentance, and forgiveness. David had great victories in his life, but he also had miserable failures and suffered greatly under the consequences of sin.

At one time, David was the most powerful man in all of Israel. As king, he possessed servants and wives and could have anything he wanted, within limits. Yet he went beyond those limits by sleeping with another man's wife. Then he attempted to cover it up by having the husband sent to the front lines of battle, where he would be killed. David paid dearly for his sin. Tragedy and heartache plagued his family for years.

The child born from the adulterous relationship died seven days after birth. Later, one of David's sons, Amnon, raped his half sister Tamar. Another son, Absalom, avenged Tamar's rape by murdering Amnon. David's household would never be the same. Absalom also plotted against David and eventually went to war to depose him. Absalom was eventually killed, adding further heartache to an already tragic story.

For years after his adulterous affair, David experienced deceit, treachery, strife, deaths in his family, and anguish. Yet he was drawn back to the Lord through God's love and mercy. Who better to be God's spokesman on betrayal, guilt, and forgiveness than King David? God used David's multifaceted human experiences to write the Psalms. David's writing gives us unparalleled insights into God's heart of love: "The LORD is compassionate and merciful, slow to get angry and filled with unfailing love" (Psalm 103:8). David's encounter with his loving Lord transformed his life. In the psalms he wrote, we see his tender heart of devotion, his desire to serve, and his deep passion to know God intimately. King David was no randomly chosen spokesman to write God's Word. He was God's powerful messenger because he had experienced God's message in his life. God knew that humanity needed the message of unfailing love conveyed through the writings of a king who knew what it was like to suffer guilt and receive forgiveness.

In other instances, God realized we would need the exalted poetry of a prophet or the priestly perspective of a theologian. Thus he conveyed his universal truths through writers who employed a variety of literary forms and styles, so that those truths would be relevant and understandable to us. No matter who we are, or how varied our human experience, God's Word has been transmitted through the perspectives, emotions, and circumstances of his spokesmen to meet our needs at just the right time.

Think about Moses' experiences and how they prepared him to be God's spokesman for the first five books of the Bible. He was born in a Hebrew home at a time when Israel was enslaved by the Egyptians and the king of Egypt (the pharaoh) was having all male Hebrew babies killed. To save Moses, his mother hid him in a basket along the Nile River. The pharaoh's daughter found him and kept him as her own. As God would have it, the princess unwittingly hired Moses' own mother to nurse the baby.

Brought up as a prince in the halls of Egyptian power, Moses was educated in all the wisdom of the Egyptians. He acquired literary skills and was trained as a leader, perhaps even groomed to be the next pharaoh. Yet seeing the plight of the Israelites under slavery, he killed an Egyptian. At the age of forty, Moses was forced to live in hiding as a shepherd. Forty more years passed before God called Moses to lead his people out of Egypt to the Promised Land. You know the story. After the pharaoh finally let the Israelites go, Moses led the wandering children of Israel in the desert for another forty years.

Here was a man who was highly educated, had known a life of royalty, murdered an Egyptian, lived as a shepherd, won freedom for his people, performed miracles, spoke directly to God, and eventually led the children of Israel to the borders of the Promised Land. He had a great mix of human experiences over his 120 years of life, and he was the ideal candidate to be God's spokesman and write his words.

He was God's perfect choice to convey the creation story, the historic beginnings of the human race, and God's covenant with his people to bring redemption and restoration to a sinful world.

The apostle Paul is another example of how God used a man's life experiences to convey precisely what God wanted us to know and what we needed to hear. At first, Paul (then known as Saul) was a leading persecutor of the early Christians. He was highly educated in Jewish law—a Hebrew of the Hebrews and a zealous Pharisee. Legalistic to a fault, he was proud and arrogant, and a tenacious and ruthless enemy of Christ. But after a life-transforming conversion, he became the passionate apostle Paul, who loved Christ and led the early church in love and humility. His unswerving devotion to Jesus often got him into trouble. He wrote many of his letters from prison. During his years of travel and ministry, he was punished by the civil authorities on several occasions—receiving thirty-nine lashes five times and being beaten with rods three times. On one occasion he was stoned, but survived, and he was shipwrecked three times, endured countless sleepless nights, and suffered hunger and thirst while leading a growing but persecuted church (see Philippians 3).

Because of Paul's background and life experiences, God could communicate effectively through him to spell out the meaning of salvation, the nature of grace, and how Christ is the center of everything. Thus we've come to understand God's heart and mind through the writings of a gifted scholar, theologian, and humble servant of Christ.

Each book, each page, and each paragraph of Scripture was written through the lens of its human spokesmen, yet it still communicates the exact message God wants us to receive. His God-breathed words were supernaturally guided through his selected human instruments so that his truth would be vivid and relevant to our lives. With God as the author and men as the writers, the sixty-six books of the Bible can rightly be called the Word of God.

There is one other question to be answered concerning inspiration. The Bible—God's Word—encompasses thirty-nine books in the Old Testament and twenty-seven books in the New Testament. Many other books and letters about God and his ways were written before the Bible was completed. How do we know that these particular books are the ones God inspired? Who decided which books would be published as the entire Holy Bible? If humans made that choice, perhaps they overlooked some God-breathed writing or included some that were not God's Word. Who's to say? That is the topic of the next chapter.

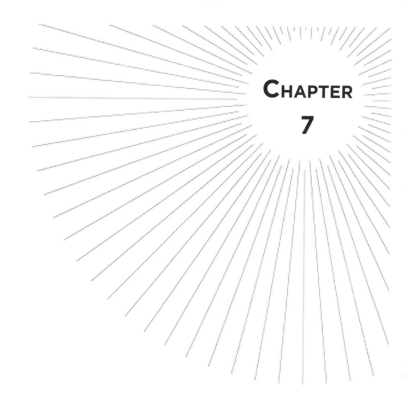

CHAPTER
7

Who Decided What Books Would Become Scripture?

"I'm so excited," the man said as he sat down to breakfast. "The new letters are supposed to arrive today."

"What letters, Father?" his son asked.

"The newly copied letters of the apostles. We have been borrowing the worn-out letters from the church in Alexandria. Now our church will have our very own set."

It was the fifth century, and this small Egyptian church was about to get the writings of Matthew, Mark, John, and Paul. Sixteen centuries later, in 2013, I acquired fragments of these letters, which I have mounted under glass. They are now tattered and faded in places. But back then, newly copied onto freshly prepared papyrus, the hand-lettered pages were crisp and sharp.

Why was this Egyptian Christian congregation so excited about getting a copy of Scripture for their very own? Why would a father, as depicted in my fictional anecdote above, be elated about the arrival of these writings? At the time, the letters of Paul and John, and the Gospels of Matthew and Mark, were not even officially recognized as Scripture. So why were these writings so cherished that they had been copied and passed down for some 250 years after they were originally written? What made them so special to this church if they were not part of an official Bible?

Matthew and Mark first wrote their narratives of Jesus' life sometime around the mid to late AD 60s. Paul wrote his letter to the church in the Roman province of Galatia in the mid to late AD 50s. John's narrative and his letters were written some thirty-five years later. In the time before these writings, the news of Jesus' death and resurrection was spread merely by word of mouth. Peter and the other disciples preached and circulated the Gospel message throughout the immediate area around Jerusalem, where Christ had been crucified and resurrected. Paul, after his conversion, began visiting and writing letters to the groups of Christ followers he met along the way. He was the most traveled of the apostles.

Antioch of Syria, the third largest city in the Roman Empire, became the hub of Paul's operation. He journeyed west of Syria to the island of Cyprus; to Galatia, which is now the western part of modern Turkey; and then to Asia Minor and Greece. Paul covered more than fifteen hundred miles in his travels. He wrote thirteen letters to the budding churches that were rapidly forming. The Gospel narratives and the letters from James, Peter, and John were also being circulated.

At first, the Gospel message was spread by the disciples by word of mouth, and the growth was primarily by addition. Peter's message on the day of Pentecost, for example, added about three thousand people to the newly birthed church. But once the apostles' writings began to be circulated, the Gospel message was transformed into a ministry of multiplication that fueled the spread of Christ's message exponentially. Small churches sprang up throughout the known world as a result of the apostles' writings. The people receiving these writings knew they had come from men who had known Jesus personally or were considered authorities on him and his teaching. Therefore they recognized that the documents being circulated were God's inspired words empowered by the very presence of the Holy Spirit.

By AD 100, the apostles had died, but the Christian church was still in its infancy, with fewer than twenty-five thousand proclaimed followers of Christ. But within the next two hundred years, the fledgling church experienced explosive multiplicative growth, to include as many as twenty million people.[1] This means the church of Jesus Christ quadrupled every generation for five consecutive generations!

Though some divisions occurred among the churches during this time, there was an amazing unity and focus of purpose and teaching. This was because every group appealed to apostolic authority. It was the writings of the apostles, or men close to and endorsed by them, that each group believed were supernaturally guided by God to reveal the teachings and truth about Jesus Christ.

The church of the fourth century recognized the authority of the apostles' writings because they sensed they were from God and that the supernatural power of God's Spirit enveloped each word. It was as if God had breathed each word personally to them. But they also relied on the insights and counsel of the church leaders who had lived during the time of the apostles. These church fathers, as they came to be called, included authoritative figures such as Clement of Rome, Ignatius, and Polycarp. These men had known the apostles and wrote extensively, confirming the authenticity and authority of the apostles' writings. This reinforced to the early church that what the apostles had written was truly from God.

Even the apostle Peter, who wrote his second letter prior to AD 64, confirmed that the letters of Paul to the churches belonged in the category of Scripture. He indicates this in 2 Peter 3:15–16. Though there was no *official* New Testament during these early years of the church, by the time the last apostle (John) died, around AD 100, there was consistent recognition among Christ followers that the twenty-seven books we now know as the New Testament were the true, inspired Word of God.

Who Really Decided?

You may have heard that an ancient church council decided which books of the Bible, namely the New Testament, were considered Scripture. But actually no one person, organization, or group determined which letters or writings of the apostles were to be granted the status of Scripture. Rather, individuals, and most notably the early church throughout the known world, *recognized* or *discovered* which books were God-breathed from their very inception. In other words, no group gave a particular writing the authority of being Scripture; the writings themselves, through the power of the Holy Spirit, made it clear that God had divinely appointed them as Scripture.

There was, however, a standard or rule established to guide the early church in its discovery of which writings were authentic, God-inspired Scripture. The discovery process led to the inclusion of a certain group of books that are referred to as the *canon* of Scripture. *Canon* comes from the Greek word *kanōn*, meaning "measuring rod" or "rule." From biblical and church history, we find at least four measurements or rules that guided the church leaders in recognizing which writings were divinely inspired:

1. The writing was authored by an apostle or prophet of God or by someone closely connected with one or more of the apostles or prophets.
2. The writings clearly evidenced the confirming power and presence of God.
3. The message was consistent with other recognized Scripture.
4. The writing was widely accepted by the church from an early date.[2]

In AD 367, Athanasius of Alexandria compiled the first official list of books that we know today as the New Testament. There were twenty-seven books listed in all. These books were then canonized officially by the church at the councils of Hippo (AD 393) and Carthage (AD 397). Again, these councils didn't *authorize* which writings were God-breathed works; rather, they *recognized* that these writings were authorized by God himself.

The Old Testament, composed of thirty-nine books, was officially recognized as God-breathed Scripture as early as the fourth century BC and certainly no later than 150 BC.[3] The Old Testament text of the thirty-nine books was originally divided into twenty-four books.

It was the same content we have today, but some of the writings that are now separate books were previously combined, thus accounting for the lower total of twenty-four. These books were originally grouped into three major divisions: five books of the Law of Moses, eight books of the Prophets, and eleven books under the umbrella designation of Writings.

The most definitive recognition that the whole of the Old Testament was God-breathed came from none other than Jesus himself. He not only quoted and repeatedly taught from the Old Testament, but he specifically referred to its three sections when he said, "Everything written about me in the law of Moses [the five books] and the prophets [the eight books] and in the Psalms [included in the eleven writings] must be fulfilled" (Luke 24:44).

Jesus also cited the entire span of the Hebrew text (our Old Testament), from its first book to its last, when he referred to the first and last martyrs within its pages. He said, "This generation will be held responsible for the murder of all God's prophets from the creation of the world—from the murder of Abel to the murder of Zechariah" (Luke 11:50–51). This was the same as saying "from Genesis to Malachi." This quote from Luke 11 clearly confirms that Jesus accepted the entire Old Testament canon.

Did God Inspire More Than Sixty-Six Books?

Have you ever felt that God ministered to you through the reading of a good book written by a Christian author or through an inspired song? Many people have written music or books throughout history that God has used to speak to us. He is alive today through the Holy Spirit, and he can guide people to write inspiring works. So did God inspire others to write his God-breathed words beyond the sixty-six books of the Bible? Is there other "Scripture" out there that is as valid as the Bible?

In short, the answer is no—because the Jewish and church leaders long ago sensed that the time of God's direct communication to us through the writings of the prophets and apostles was closed. The period of about fifteen hundred years that is recognized as the span of God's special revelation extends from the time of Moses to the death of John, the last apostle.

During this time, God revealed himself in a special and direct way. The writer of the book of Hebrews puts it like this: "Long ago God spoke many times and in many ways to our ancestors through the prophets. And now in these final days, he has spoken to us through his Son" (Hebrews 1:1–2). Once God had delivered his complete message through his prophets and through Jesus, he "closed the book," so to speak, on God-breathed inspiration. This isn't to say that God hasn't blessed the many writings of various God-anointed people down through the years. But those writings do not rise to the level of God's authoritative Word.

During the time the canonical books were being written, other spiritual writings surfaced that some leaders thought might be considered God-breathed Scripture. In fact, some apostles even quoted from these writings. In the short book that bears his name, Jude quotes from 1 Enoch 1:9 (Jude 1:14–15). Yet the Jewish leaders did not consider the book of Enoch to be part of Scripture.

Fourteen books emerged as spiritual writings that some thought should be included as Scripture in the Old Testament. Now called the Apocrypha, these added books surfaced between 200 BC and the early second century AD. They include

- First Esdras
- Second Esdras
- Tobit
- Judith

- Additions to Esther
- The Wisdom of Solomon
- Ecclesiasticus
- Baruch
- Susanna
- Bel and the Dragon (additions to Daniel)
- The Song of the Three Hebrew Children (additions to Daniel)
- The Prayer of Manasseh
- First Maccabees
- Second Maccabees

Some people believe these fourteen books should be added to the twenty-four canonized books of the Hebrew text, and some have added them to the Greek Septuagint translation of the Old Testament. The Jewish leaders, however, recognized only the original twenty-four books of the Hebrew text as Scripture—the same books Jesus had confirmed. Also, it can be noted that Jesus never quoted from any of the added fourteen books. He cited only from the twenty-four books recognized as the Jewish canon—the same reordered thirty-nine books we have today. Luke 24:27 uses the phrase "all the Scriptures" when referring to the Old Testament, which confirms that Jesus accepted the same complete Hebrew books that Judaism recognized as canonical at the time.

Today these fourteen books are still in existence and are referred to as the Apocrypha, which means "that which is hidden." Though these books were not accepted by the early church or the Jewish scholars as late as 150 BC, they were eventually included in the Old Testament by the Roman Catholic Church in AD 1546.

The Protestant Bible does not include the Apocrypha in the Old Testament for the reasons cited above. Protestant scholars also point out that none of the fourteen books of the Apocrypha claims divine inspiration. In fact, some actually disclaim inspiration. They also explain that highly respected Jewish philosophers such as Philo Judaeus of Alexandria, historians such as Josephus, and translators such as the renowned Jerome, as well as the early church fathers, rejected the Apocrypha as God-breathed Scripture.

Though the twenty-seven books of the New Testament were unofficially recognized as Scripture by the church as early as AD 100, some wondered whether certain other spiritual writings were also God-breathed. By the middle of the second century, a number of writings emerged, known as the New Testament Apocrypha and Gnostic writings. These include the Infancy Gospel of Thomas, the Gospel of Thomas, the Gospel of Peter, and the Gospel of Judas.

These writings by and large contradict the Gospels of Matthew, Mark, Luke, and John and Paul's epistles. Some of their contradictory teachings include the idea that there were multiple creators; that salvation is by "spiritual knowledge"; that ignorance, not sin, is humanity's problem; and other teachings that were refuted in the twenty-seven books of the New Testament. The Infancy Gospel of Thomas, a Gnostic writing, depicts a scene in which a young Jesus reacts to being bumped into by some children by striking them down with his supernatural power.

All of these added spiritual writings were rejected by the early church and were, in part, why the church fathers established a set of rules in the first place for recognizing which writings were truly inspired by God.

Today, we can know with confidence that the thirty-nine books of the Old Testament and the twenty-seven books of the New Testament are God's complete message to us. Though we can gain from other writings of spiritually gifted men and women, we can rest assured that what we have in our Bibles today is what God wants us to know.

Aside from being recognized as God-breathed Scripture, these sixty-six books stand out because they are unique in many other ways. When you stand back and compare these writings with others, you realize that the Bible is a one-of-a-kind book, unlike any other in all antiquity. That uniqueness is the subject of our next chapter.

CHAPTER
8

Unique: One of a Kind

Left: A modern-day scribe copies the Hebrew Scriptures.

Immediately below: Gallnuts were used to produce ink and treat skin panels (parchments) to create a scroll.

Below: Closer examination of the Lodz Torah dated between AD 1450-1500.

Close-up view of columns 1-6 of the Lodz Torah.

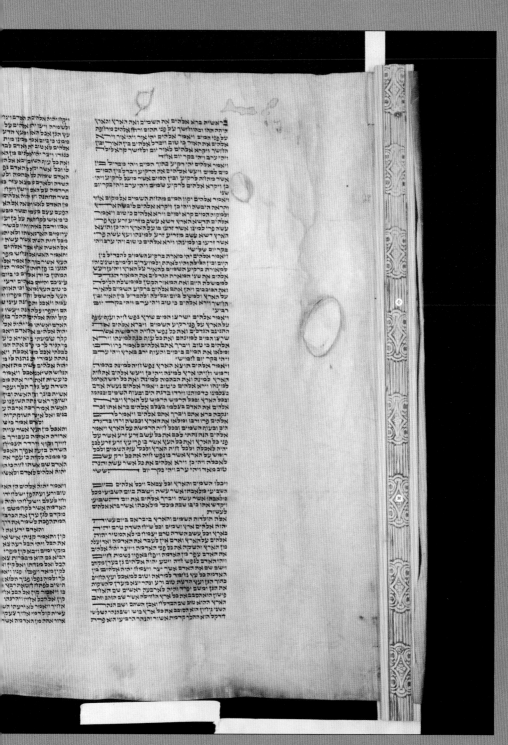

בְּרֵאשִׁית בָּרָא אֱלֹהִים אֵת הַשָּׁמַיִם וְאֵת הָאָרֶץ וְהָאָרֶץ הָיְתָה תֹהוּ וָבֹהוּ וְחֹשֶׁךְ עַל פְּנֵי תְהוֹם וְרוּחַ אֱלֹהִים מְרַחֶפֶת עַל פְּנֵי הַמָּיִם וַיֹּאמֶר אֱלֹהִים יְהִי אוֹר וַיְהִי אוֹר וַיַּרְא אֱלֹהִים אֶת הָאוֹר כִּי טוֹב וַיַּבְדֵּל אֱלֹהִים בֵּין הָאוֹר וּבֵין הַחֹשֶׁךְ וַיִּקְרָא אֱלֹהִים לָאוֹר יוֹם וְלַחֹשֶׁךְ קָרָא לָיְלָה וַיְהִי עֶרֶב וַיְהִי בֹקֶר יוֹם אֶחָד

וַיֹּאמֶר אֱלֹהִים יְהִי רָקִיעַ בְּתוֹךְ הַמָּיִם וִיהִי מַבְדִּיל בֵּין מַיִם לָמָיִם וַיַּעַשׂ אֱלֹהִים אֶת הָרָקִיעַ וַיַּבְדֵּל בֵּין הַמַּיִם אֲשֶׁר מִתַּחַת לָרָקִיעַ וּבֵין הַמַּיִם אֲשֶׁר מֵעַל לָרָקִיעַ וַיְהִי כֵן וַיִּקְרָא אֱלֹהִים לָרָקִיעַ שָׁמָיִם וַיְהִי עֶרֶב וַיְהִי בֹקֶר יוֹם שֵׁנִי

וַיֹּאמֶר אֱלֹהִים יִקָּווּ הַמַּיִם מִתַּחַת הַשָּׁמַיִם אֶל מָקוֹם אֶחָד וְתֵרָאֶה הַיַּבָּשָׁה וַיְהִי כֵן וַיִּקְרָא אֱלֹהִים לַיַּבָּשָׁה אֶרֶץ וּלְמִקְוֵה הַמַּיִם קָרָא יַמִּים וַיַּרְא אֱלֹהִים כִּי טוֹב וַיֹּאמֶר אֱלֹהִים תַּדְשֵׁא הָאָרֶץ דֶּשֶׁא עֵשֶׂב מַזְרִיעַ זֶרַע עֵץ פְּרִי עֹשֶׂה פְּרִי לְמִינוֹ אֲשֶׁר זַרְעוֹ בוֹ עַל הָאָרֶץ וַיְהִי כֵן וַתּוֹצֵא הָאָרֶץ דֶּשֶׁא עֵשֶׂב מַזְרִיעַ זֶרַע לְמִינֵהוּ וְעֵץ עֹשֶׂה פְּרִי אֲשֶׁר זַרְעוֹ בוֹ לְמִינֵהוּ וַיַּרְא אֱלֹהִים כִּי טוֹב וַיְהִי עֶרֶב וַיְהִי בֹקֶר יוֹם שְׁלִישִׁי

וַיֹּאמֶר אֱלֹהִים יְהִי מְאֹרֹת בִּרְקִיעַ הַשָּׁמַיִם לְהַבְדִּיל בֵּין הַיּוֹם וּבֵין הַלָּיְלָה וְהָיוּ לְאֹתֹת וּלְמוֹעֲדִים וּלְיָמִים וְשָׁנִים וְהָיוּ לִמְאוֹרֹת בִּרְקִיעַ הַשָּׁמַיִם לְהָאִיר עַל הָאָרֶץ וַיְהִי כֵן וַיַּעַשׂ אֱלֹהִים אֶת שְׁנֵי הַמְּאֹרֹת הַגְּדֹלִים אֶת הַמָּאוֹר הַגָּדֹל לְמֶמְשֶׁלֶת הַיּוֹם וְאֶת הַמָּאוֹר הַקָּטֹן לְמֶמְשֶׁלֶת הַלַּיְלָה וְאֵת הַכּוֹכָבִים וַיִּתֵּן אֹתָם אֱלֹהִים בִּרְקִיעַ הַשָּׁמָיִם לְהָאִיר עַל הָאָרֶץ וְלִמְשֹׁל בַּיּוֹם וּבַלַּיְלָה וּלְהַבְדִּיל בֵּין הָאוֹר וּבֵין הַחֹשֶׁךְ וַיַּרְא אֱלֹהִים כִּי טוֹב וַיְהִי עֶרֶב וַיְהִי בֹקֶר יוֹם רְבִיעִי

וַיֹּאמֶר אֱלֹהִים יִשְׁרְצוּ הַמַּיִם שֶׁרֶץ נֶפֶשׁ חַיָּה וְעוֹף יְעוֹפֵף עַל הָאָרֶץ עַל פְּנֵי רְקִיעַ הַשָּׁמָיִם וַיִּבְרָא אֱלֹהִים אֶת הַתַּנִּינִם הַגְּדֹלִים וְאֵת כָּל נֶפֶשׁ הַחַיָּה הָרֹמֶשֶׂת אֲשֶׁר שָׁרְצוּ הַמַּיִם לְמִינֵהֶם וְאֵת כָּל עוֹף כָּנָף לְמִינֵהוּ וַיַּרְא אֱלֹהִים כִּי טוֹב וַיְבָרֶךְ אֹתָם אֱלֹהִים לֵאמֹר פְּרוּ וּרְבוּ וּמִלְאוּ אֶת הַמַּיִם בַּיַּמִּים וְהָעוֹף יִרֶב בָּאָרֶץ וַיְהִי עֶרֶב וַיְהִי בֹקֶר יוֹם חֲמִישִׁי

וַיֹּאמֶר אֱלֹהִים תּוֹצֵא הָאָרֶץ נֶפֶשׁ חַיָּה לְמִינָהּ בְּהֵמָה וָרֶמֶשׂ וְחַיְתוֹ אֶרֶץ לְמִינָהּ וַיְהִי כֵן וַיַּעַשׂ אֱלֹהִים אֶת חַיַּת הָאָרֶץ לְמִינָהּ וְאֶת הַבְּהֵמָה לְמִינָהּ וְאֵת כָּל רֶמֶשׂ הָאֲדָמָה לְמִינֵהוּ וַיַּרְא אֱלֹהִים כִּי טוֹב וַיֹּאמֶר אֱלֹהִים נַעֲשֶׂה אָדָם בְּצַלְמֵנוּ כִּדְמוּתֵנוּ וְיִרְדּוּ בִדְגַת הַיָּם וּבְעוֹף הַשָּׁמַיִם וּבַבְּהֵמָה וּבְכָל הָאָרֶץ וּבְכָל הָרֶמֶשׂ הָרֹמֵשׂ עַל הָאָרֶץ וַיִּבְרָא אֱלֹהִים אֶת הָאָדָם בְּצַלְמוֹ בְּצֶלֶם אֱלֹהִים בָּרָא אֹתוֹ זָכָר וּנְקֵבָה בָּרָא אֹתָם וַיְבָרֶךְ אֹתָם אֱלֹהִים וַיֹּאמֶר לָהֶם אֱלֹהִים פְּרוּ וּרְבוּ וּמִלְאוּ אֶת הָאָרֶץ וְכִבְשֻׁהָ וּרְדוּ בִּדְגַת הַיָּם וּבְעוֹף הַשָּׁמַיִם וּבְכָל חַיָּה הָרֹמֶשֶׂת עַל הָאָרֶץ וַיֹּאמֶר אֱלֹהִים הִנֵּה נָתַתִּי לָכֶם אֶת כָּל עֵשֶׂב זֹרֵעַ זֶרַע אֲשֶׁר עַל פְּנֵי כָל הָאָרֶץ וְאֶת כָּל הָעֵץ אֲשֶׁר בּוֹ פְרִי עֵץ זֹרֵעַ זָרַע לָכֶם יִהְיֶה לְאָכְלָה וּלְכָל חַיַּת הָאָרֶץ וּלְכָל עוֹף הַשָּׁמַיִם וּלְכֹל רוֹמֵשׂ עַל הָאָרֶץ אֲשֶׁר בּוֹ נֶפֶשׁ חַיָּה אֶת כָּל יֶרֶק עֵשֶׂב לְאָכְלָה וַיְהִי כֵן וַיַּרְא אֱלֹהִים אֶת כָּל אֲשֶׁר עָשָׂה וְהִנֵּה טוֹב מְאֹד וַיְהִי עֶרֶב וַיְהִי בֹקֶר יוֹם הַשִּׁשִּׁי

וַיְכֻלּוּ הַשָּׁמַיִם וְהָאָרֶץ וְכָל צְבָאָם וַיְכַל אֱלֹהִים בַּיּוֹם הַשְּׁבִיעִי מְלַאכְתּוֹ אֲשֶׁר עָשָׂה וַיִּשְׁבֹּת בַּיּוֹם הַשְּׁבִיעִי מִכָּל מְלַאכְתּוֹ אֲשֶׁר עָשָׂה וַיְבָרֶךְ אֱלֹהִים אֶת יוֹם הַשְּׁבִיעִי וַיְקַדֵּשׁ אֹתוֹ כִּי בוֹ שָׁבַת מִכָּל מְלַאכְתּוֹ אֲשֶׁר בָּרָא אֱלֹהִים לַעֲשׂוֹת

אֵלֶּה תוֹלְדוֹת הַשָּׁמַיִם וְהָאָרֶץ בְּהִבָּרְאָם בְּיוֹם עֲשׂוֹת יְהוָה אֱלֹהִים אֶרֶץ וְשָׁמָיִם וְכֹל שִׂיחַ הַשָּׂדֶה טֶרֶם יִהְיֶה בָאָרֶץ וְכָל עֵשֶׂב הַשָּׂדֶה טֶרֶם יִצְמָח כִּי לֹא הִמְטִיר יְהוָה אֱלֹהִים עַל הָאָרֶץ וְאָדָם אַיִן לַעֲבֹד אֶת הָאֲדָמָה וְאֵד יַעֲלֶה מִן הָאָרֶץ וְהִשְׁקָה אֶת כָּל פְּנֵי הָאֲדָמָה וַיִּיצֶר יְהוָה אֱלֹהִים אֶת הָאָדָם עָפָר מִן הָאֲדָמָה וַיִּפַּח בְּאַפָּיו נִשְׁמַת חַיִּים וַיְהִי הָאָדָם לְנֶפֶשׁ חַיָּה וַיִּטַּע יְהוָה אֱלֹהִים גַּן בְּעֵדֶן מִקֶּדֶם וַיָּשֶׂם שָׁם אֶת הָאָדָם אֲשֶׁר יָצָר וַיַּצְמַח יְהוָה אֱלֹהִים מִן הָאֲדָמָה כָּל עֵץ נֶחְמָד לְמַרְאֶה וְטוֹב לְמַאֲכָל וְעֵץ הַחַיִּים בְּתוֹךְ הַגָּן וְעֵץ הַדַּעַת טוֹב וָרָע וְנָהָר יֹצֵא מֵעֵדֶן לְהַשְׁקוֹת אֶת הַגָּן וּמִשָּׁם יִפָּרֵד וְהָיָה לְאַרְבָּעָה רָאשִׁים שֵׁם הָאֶחָד פִּישׁוֹן הוּא הַסֹּבֵב אֵת כָּל אֶרֶץ הַחֲוִילָה אֲשֶׁר שָׁם הַזָּהָב וּזְהַב הָאָרֶץ הַהִוא טוֹב שָׁם הַבְּדֹלַח וְאֶבֶן הַשֹּׁהַם וְשֵׁם הַנָּהָר הַשֵּׁנִי גִּיחוֹן הוּא הַסּוֹבֵב אֵת כָּל אֶרֶץ כּוּשׁ וְשֵׁם הַנָּהָר הַשְּׁלִישִׁי חִדֶּקֶל הוּא הַהֹלֵךְ קִדְמַת אַשּׁוּר וְהַנָּהָר הָרְבִיעִי הוּא פְרָת

Top & Left: The Lodz Torah rolled out and rolled up.

Below: Egyptian burial mask.

Seven unpublished papyrus fragments perhaps dating as far back as AD 350.

Matthew 6:33

Matthew 7:4

Jeremiah 33:24

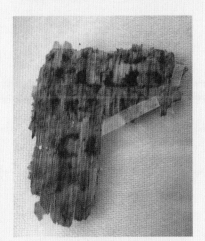
Galatians 4:17

Mark 15:9

1 John 2:21

John 14:28

Discover the Evidence Event,
December 2013: Examining
papyrus fragments just extracted
from ancient artifacts.

Discover the Evidence event, December 2013: Carefully extracting papyrus fragments and then trying to initially identify the writings.

Unique—being the only one;
being without a like or equal: unequaled.[1]

How many books are there in the world? A few years ago, the Google Books Library Project came up with an answer. According to Leonid Taycher, a Google software engineer who at the time worked on the project, there are 129,864,880 books in the world.[2] And we're talking about number of titles, not number of copies of all titles. Out of these almost 130 million books, there is one that is truly unique. It stands out as being the only one of its kind. It is unequaled. It is the Bible.

No other book is God-breathed. No other book is a collection of writings that are the very thoughts and concepts of God. The Bible is the only one that carries that distinction. We can add to that distinction at least four other unequaled characteristics of the Bible: God's Word is unique in its continuity; its translation; its circulation; and its survival through time, persecution, and criticism.

Looking at each of these unique characteristics of the Bible can give us a renewed sense of awe and appreciation of God's Word.

The Bible Is Unique in Its Continuity

We have mentioned before that the Bible was written over a span of fifteen hundred years by more than forty different writers from practically every walk of life. They wrote in different places at various times during different moods. Some wrote from the heights of joy; others wrote from the depths of despair. Some wrote during times of certainty and conviction, while others wrote out of confusion and doubt. The Bible was written on three different continents (Asia, Africa, and Europe) in three different languages (Hebrew, Aramaic, and Greek).

Now consider the wide variety of literary styles found in the Bible, including poetry, song, romance, personal correspondence, memories, diaries, biography, autobiography, prophecy, historical narrative, law, didactic treatise, satire, parable, and allegory. Within these literary styles, the writers address hundreds of controversial subjects. Yet from the first word of Genesis to the last word of Revelation, the Bible communicates an amazing harmony of thought and avoids contradicting itself.

How could any book developed over such a long period of time with such diverse writers, styles, subjects, and views not be filled with conflicting and contradictory positions and perspectives? One would expect such a book to be inevitably disjointed and inconsistent. This would certainly be the case if the book's true author were not God himself. The Bible stands out as one of a kind in its continuity and harmony of theme, because it is God's book.

From Adam and Eve's choice in the Garden of Eden to God's response, a single plan emerges. From the giving of the Law to Moses to the sacrifices of lambs and goats, one purpose stands out. From a sinless baby in a manger to a holy sacrifice on a cruel cross, one mission becomes clear. From the resurrection of Christ to the promise to restore a sinful world to the Creator's original design, every chapter of every book in the Bible cries out with one voice—*God's*—and one relational theme: *redemption!* God has gone to extraordinary lengths through the incarnation of Jesus to redeem and restore his lost children to himself. God is passionate about his relationship with the human race, and his Word, empowered by the Holy Spirit, is his means to communicate the good news of his redemptive plan. The Bible is truly unique in its continuity.

The Bible Is Unique in Its Translation

The Old Testament was first translated from Hebrew and Aramaic into Greek around 250 BC to 150 BC. The Septuagint version was primarily what the Greek-speaking world read during the time of

Jesus. Later, other scholars translated the Old Testament into Greek as well. Their translation, the Coptic version, was completed around AD 350. Coptic is a version of Late Egyptian that was written in mostly Greek characters. The Latin Vulgate was translated by the scholar Jerome beginning in AD 382. It took him twenty-five years to complete the project. The Vulgate version of Scripture was the first major book that Johannes Gutenberg published on his brand-new printing press in 1455.

By the beginning of the fourth century, the Hebrew and Greek Bibles had been translated into languages such as Slavic, Syriac (a late version of Aramaic), Armenian, Bohairic (a dialect of Coptic), Persian, Arabic, Frankish, and Anglo-Saxon.

Bible translations into English, or its precursor languages, began in the fifth century with the Anglo-Saxon version. The first translator to render the entire Bible in English was John Wycliffe (1329–1384). His English translation was the only English Bible for 145 years. William Tyndale, perhaps the greatest of modern English translators of the Bible, created the Tyndale version of the English Bible in 1525. One of the most popular versions in the English-speaking world, and still popular today, is the well-known Authorized Version, better known as the King James Version (1611).

The process of translating the Bible into different languages began as early as 250 BC to 150 BC and continues today. The Bible is now the most translated book of all time. The United Bible Societies reports that, as of 2014, the Bible or portions of the Bible have been translated into 2,650 languages. Their Digital Bible Library now hosts more than eight hundred translations in 636 languages spoken by 4.3 billion people. The many languages into which the Bible has been translated encompass the primary modes of communication for well over 90 percent of the world's population.[3] The Bible is truly unique in its translation.

The Bible Is Unique in Its Circulation

Every author would love to have his or her book hit the *New York Times* Bestseller list. For any book to reach sales of one hundred thousand is rare, and it's even rarer to hit sales of one million books. The Bible, however, has no equal. Distribution of the Bible is now into the billions of copies! More copies of the Bible and selected portions of the Bible are in circulation than any other book in history.

According to a report from the United Bible Societies, they distributed 32.1 million full Bibles and more than 372 million selections from the Bible in 2012 alone.[4] The Bible is truly unique in its circulation.

The Bible Is Unique in Its Survival through Time, Persecution, and Criticism

Scripture was written on perishable materials, so it had to be copied and recopied for many hundreds of years before the invention of the printing press. Yet both the Old and New Testament documents have survived through time like no other writing in history. Compared with other ancient writings, the Bible has more manuscript evidence to support it than the top ten pieces of classical literature combined.[5]

The Bible has survived not only through time, but also through great persecution. In AD 303, the Roman emperor Diocletian issued an edict to stop Christians from worshipping and to destroy their Scriptures. "An imperial letter was everywhere promulgated, ordering the razing of the churches to the ground and the destruction by fire of the Scriptures, and proclaiming that those who held high positions would lose all civil rights, while those in households, if they persisted in their profession of Christianity, would be deprived of their liberty."[6]

The historic irony of this event is recorded by Eusebius, a fourth-century church historian, who writes that twenty-five years after Diocletian's edict, the Roman emperor Constantine ordered fifty copies of the Scriptures to be prepared at the government's expense.[7]

Since the time the original manuscripts of Scripture were written, many attempts have been made to destroy the Bible. However, God's Word has not only prevailed but also proliferated. Voltaire, the noted eighteenth-century French writer and skeptic, predicted that within a hundred years of his time, Christianity would be but a footnote in history. Voltaire is long gone, yet God's Word has lived on for centuries. "People are like grass that dies away," the apostle Peter writes, quoting the prophet Isaiah, "but the word of the Lord will last forever" (1 Peter 1:24–25).

The Bible has withstood the sands of time and the efforts of those who wished to stamp it out. It has also endured through harsh criticism.

Noted nineteenth-century scholar and writer H. L. Hastings forcefully states the unique way in which the Bible has withstood attacks of infidels and skeptics:

> *Infidels for eighteen hundred years have been refuting and overthrowing this book, and yet it stands today as solid as a rock. Its circulation increases, and it is more loved and cherished and read today than ever before. Infidels, with all their assaults, make about as much impression on this book as a man with a tack hammer would on the Pyramids of Egypt. . . . If this book had not been the book of God, men would have destroyed it long ago. Emperors and popes, kings and priests, princes and rulers have all tried their hand at it; they die and the book still lives.[8]*

Theologian and apologist Bernard Ramm, speaking of how the Bible has come under criticism, put it this way:

> *No other book has been so chopped, knived, sifted, scrutinized, and vilified. What book on philosophy or*

*religion or psychology or belles lettres of classical or modern
times has been subject to such a mass attack as the Bible?
with such venom and skepticism? with such thoroughness
and erudition? upon every chapter, line and tenet?*

*The Bible is still loved by millions, read by millions,
and studied by millions.*[9]

Over thousands of years, the Bible has been tried and tested and is truly unique in its survival through time, persecution, and criticism.

Here, however, is an interesting thought. Being unique—as the Bible is—doesn't actually make it true. So in the next section, I would like you to journey with me to discover why we have assurance that the Bible is true. We will explore the undeniable reliability of God's powerful Word. Knowing that God's Word is trustworthy will truly deepen your faith in its Author and in its universal truths.

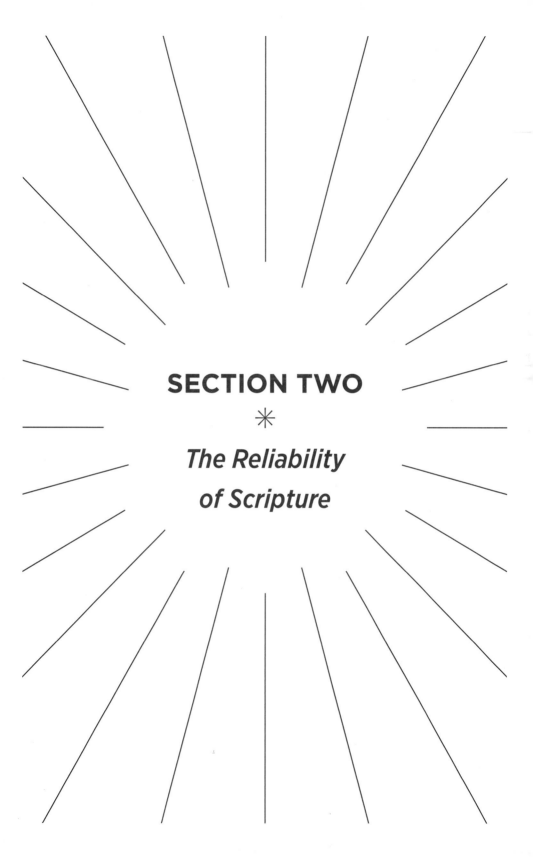

SECTION TWO

✳

*The Reliability
of Scripture*

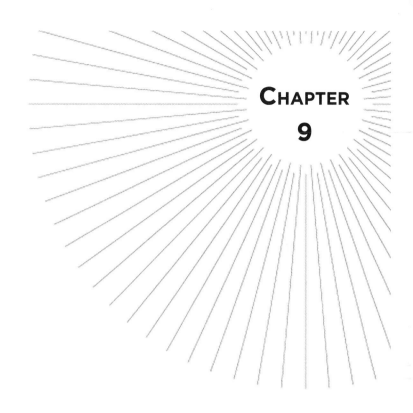

CHAPTER
9

Before the Printing Press

Imagine an impoverished Jewish community in a small town in Poland in the mid-1400s, long before Mozart ever wrote a note, before Martin Luther launched the Reformation, before Sir Isaac Newton discovered the primary laws of physics, and even before Christopher Columbus sailed for India and instead discovered America. Something is about to take place in this poor community that will ripple through the centuries. Perhaps it happened like this:

It was nearing midnight when the Jewish scribe Baruch was startled by a sudden knock on his door.

Who could possibly be calling at this late hour?

Baruch's heart began to pound like a hammer. Cautiously, hesitantly, he opened the door. . .and stepped back quickly as a figure out of the darkness burst into his home.

"Moshe!" cried Baruch when he had recovered his senses. "What is wrong? What brings you here so late? And why are you grinning as if you had suddenly inherited a fortune?"

"Baruch, it is certified!" Moshe exclaimed. "I simply could not wait to tell you."

Moshe's elation spread immediately to Baruch. He knew exactly what Moshe meant. His friend was bringing him the news he had been hoping to hear for many weeks. The rabbi had just certified the Torah that Baruch had been copying for more than a year. The 304,805 words he had copied from Genesis to Deuteronomy were a work of art as far as the rabbi was concerned.

During the following *Shabbat* (the Jewish Sabbath), Baruch spoke to those gathered at the synagogue in their small village.

"I can proudly announce to all of you," he began, pointing to the Torah, "that our new Torah is complete! It has been certified by our rabbi." The Jewish congregation was overwhelmed with emotion.

It was easy for me to visualize such a scene, because more than 550 years later, I, too, was overwhelmed with emotion as I touched the edge of that very same Torah. I was now the owner—more precisely, I was the caretaker—of not simply a medieval Hebrew manuscript, but of a unique, complete Torah (the Jewish term for the first five books of the Old Testament). I named it the Lodz Torah in honor and memory of the more than 230,000 Jews from the Polish city of Lodz who suffered and died at the hands of the Nazis during World War II.

At that time, Lodz was the second largest city in Poland. During the war, the Jewish section of the city became known as the Lodz Ghetto, one of the largest Jewish detention camps in German-occupied Europe. This ancient scroll had been preserved through the centuries and remained the synagogue reading copy of twentieth-century Jews in Poland. I thought it fitting to name it after a group of people who had such reverence for God's Word and preserved it through such persecution. But when I received this scroll, I had no idea how rare an item I had acquired.

This Torah is rare not only because of its age, dated between AD 1450 and AD 1500, but also because of the way it was copied. Like all of its predecessors, the Lodz Torah had a rare group of *sofers* (scribes) who took great care in copying each manuscript. All scribes in ancient times took great pride in carefully hand-replicating manuscripts. But there was something special about Jewish scribes in particular. Because of the stringent rules and disciplines these scribes were required to follow, no other work in all literature has been so carefully and accurately copied as the Old Testament.

The particular discipline and art of the Jewish scribes came out of a class of Jewish scholars between the fifth and third centuries BC. They were called the *Sopherim*, from a Hebrew word meaning "scribes." The Sopherim, who initiated a stringent standard of meticulous discipline, were subsequently eclipsed by the Talmudic scribes, who guarded, interpreted, and commented on the sacred texts from AD 100 to AD 500. In turn, the Talmudic scribes were followed by the better-known and even more meticulous Masoretic scribes (AD 500–900).

The zeal of these Jewish scribes, with their stringent disciplines and rigorous attention to detail, gave their copy reproductions of Scripture equal authority to that of the parent copies. The rules, rituals, procedures, and repeated checks enabled the scribes to be thoroughly convinced that each completed copy of the Torah was an exact duplicate of previous copies. The scribe who copied the Lodz Torah followed these strict rules, for he was very much aware that he was copying God-breathed words.

The Case of the Meticulous Lodz Scribe

The Lodz Torah was written on thirty-six calfskin parchments or panels. When completely rolled out, it measures just over seventy-two feet long. It is in amazingly good condition, but that alone is not what makes it so rare.

Because the original Jewish caretakers of this Torah were from a poor community, they couldn't afford to commission a new copy when this one suffered damage. So, over the years, they hired scribes to patch it up, make any corrections, and re-ink areas in order to keep it in perfect condition.

Re-inking fading letters

Normally, a deteriorating and fading Hebrew scroll would be stored away when a new one was completed. That didn't happen with the Lodz Torah, making it an unusually old complete Torah. Because of its dating, the region it was from, the use of earlier writing traditions, and other internal factors, I had acquired a manuscript that would normally be placed alongside those found in the largest private collections of Hebrew scrolls in the entire world.

Once the background of the manuscript was researched and thoroughly analyzed, I realized what a unique and amazing treasure had come into my possession. I felt a deep responsibility to share this treasure with the world. The very existence of the scroll has for us a significant message about how and why God preserved his Word.

The Lodz Torah as it survives today was prepared predominantly by a dedicated Ashkenazi scribe some 550 years ago. Several sheets were replaced over time by four other scribes. These scribes were likely from the same family or certainly knew each other's families. From one generation to the next, they carefully preserved God's Word.

Baruch, as I am calling the fifteenth-century copyist in my story, was a scribe who precisely observed the Jewish traditions and requirements for preparing the skins and ink used in copying the Scriptures. He was certainly a rigorously trained, highly skilled, passionate professional who was highly respected in his community as a religious scholar. His work was eye-straining and backbreaking. He worked hours on end, hunched over a table, copying Scripture painstakingly in a room dimly lit by candles or oil lamps.

Baruch had talent, discipline, and extreme reverence for God's Word. He replicated each letter from an existing certified medieval Hebrew manuscript in order to create this particular Torah. To be certified as a scribe, Baruch had to memorize four thousand different laws and principles dictating how to copy Scripture in order to help ensure its accuracy. Without knowing each of these laws of manuscript transcription, he would not be qualified to copy the sacred text. Let's follow Baruch as he goes about his all-important task.

To begin, Baruch obtained ceremonially clean animal skins from a Jewish butcher and barley leaves from the market. He then cut the skins into rectangular panels. Each of these panels was soaked in water mixed with barley leaves. This procedure softened the skins, making it easier for the scribe to scrape off the hair and fibers.

Before he scraped off the hair, Baruch put the skins through several additional processes to make the scraping easier and the skins smoother. He also made a trip into the woods to gather a substance known as gallnuts—nodules that grow on the trunks of certain trees (like oak trees) and are a good source of tannin. With a razor-sharp blade and the precision of a surgeon, he cut the galls from the tree bark until he had harvested a bag full of them.

Gallnuts

Scribes have gathered gallnuts from the woods for thousands of years. These "nuts" were important to the meticulous process of creating skin panels for writing. The scribe soaked the nuts in scalding water for about six hours, causing them to release tannin, an acidic chemical compound used to treat the skins. This tanning process produced skins smooth enough to write on. The scribe then scraped and sanded each skin until it was perfectly smooth. It took him days to prepare the skin panels for writing.

Once Baruch carefully trimmed the skins into uniform rectangles, he made tiny pinpricks along the edges of the panels. He carefully placed a small dowel pin about the size of a toothpick into each of the holes, in preparation for marking the skins with a grid of symmetrical rows and columns.

Next, he strung tight threads horizontally from one dowel pin to the other. Using the threads as guides, he took a dull knife that would not cut through the skin and carefully scored the surface horizontally. This indented the skin slightly to form a distinguishable line. After lining the entire skin horizontally, he repeated the same process vertically, creating a perfect grid on which to copy each and every one of the 304,805 letters of God's written Word.

In the Western world, we write above the lines. Baruch instead, like all Jewish scribes, hung the letters from the lines.

In other words, he wrote below the lines, and he always wrote from right to left. This technique of writing below the lines means that when we look at the scroll, it appears to us in the twenty-first century to be upside down.

The grid was very important to the scribe. It kept him from weaving his letters up and down the scroll as he wrote. This process enabled him to be more accurate in copying each letter. He wanted a reader of Scripture not only to read each word accurately, but also to pronounce each word accurately. Baruch believed, like all the Jewish scribes before him, that he had a solemn responsibility to reproduce every letter perfectly and clearly. Hanging his letters on the grid aided him in accomplishing this goal. He knew that miscopying what God said could mean misreading, mispronouncing, or, worse, misinterpreting and misunderstanding what God wants his people to know about him and his ways.

Once each panel was fully written on, Baruch sewed the skins together with strings created from strips of cured and treated tendons (sinews) from the legs of a kosher calf. When this process was completed, the result was a seventy-two-foot-long scroll.

Baruch's next task was to prepare his ink and quills for writing. Remember, he had 304,805 letters to form, and not one of them was to touch another. The meticulous care and deliberation required meant it would take him more than a year to complete this beautiful Torah.

Baruch obtained a number of goose feathers as his quills. Goose feathers were generally preferred because they were firmer than other feathers and remained sharp longer. The sharper the quill, the less chance of the ink blotting and letters potentially touching each other. If either of these mishaps occurred, it would be considered an error and require correction.

In addition to the sharp feather quill, the ink Baruch used was critical to his task. Again, gallnuts were part of his formula. The process entailed crushing and soaking gallnuts and a carefully prepared mixture of items to be sure he had an ink that wouldn't fade.

As we have mentioned, a Torah scroll that began to deteriorate and fade would typically be "retired," stored away, and then burned. It would be placed in a special wooden cupboard called a *genizah*. The newly copied Torah would then become the authoritative text for the synagogue. The rabbis did not want to take a chance that a faded word would be mispronounced, misread, or misinterpreted.

The Lodz Torah, however, copied by an Ashkenazi scribe, is

the exception to this rule. It was saved centuries past its prime. As evidence of this, the ink has turned orange in places. Normally, it would have been retired to the genizah, but because this particular Jewish community couldn't afford a new copy, they hired scribes to re-ink the fading letters.

One thing that is apparent about this Torah is that it was copied from an older Torah produced during medieval times. There is clear evidence that the scribe kept many of the late-medieval scribal aspects. You can see curled letters and numerous spiral and wrapped letters that were used only during the medieval time period. This Torah also retains an early tradition for text layout. It does not conform to later models for each column, which varied in width and number of lines.

You can see that later generations of scribes, sometime after AD 1450, made notations and "corrections" to this scroll. They brought uniformity to how the text was laid out and proper orthography related to the precise writing of each letter using specific shapes and forms—even down to such details as which way a letter was to be struck with the inked quill. You can see where the scribe attempted to correct some of the earlier medieval writing traditions by applying the newer, more stringent standards.

As the rabbis of ensuing generations read this Torah, they undoubtedly understood they were encountering an earlier iteration of the sacred word. As the congregation saw it being taken out of the cabinet, it was no doubt clear to them that it was old. There were probably stories associated with how this Torah had been handed down from one generation to another. This would have reminded them of the rich historical tradition of the Scriptures.

Not Even the Tiniest of Letters Will Disappear

Every word and letter in the Hebrew text (the Old Testament) is important, just as they are in the New Testament. The apostle Paul makes it clear that "the law was our guardian until Christ came" (Galatians 3:24 NIV). Jesus himself made it clear that *he* was the fulfillment of the Old Testament promises and prophecies. That means he had not come to do away with the Old Testament: "Don't misunderstand why I have come. I did not come to abolish the law of Moses or the writings of the prophets. No, I came to accomplish their purpose" (Matthew 5:17). The Torah recounts how humans sinned against God and what that sin did to the human race. It also chronicles the covenant that God made with Abraham to redeem his people by a sacrifice to satisfy the demands of justice in dealing with our sin. Jesus became that perfect sacrificial Lamb (see Hebrews 3–10).

Jesus wanted to assure us beyond a shadow of doubt that he was the completion of God's law and that his Word would last forever, down to the last detail. So he said, "For assuredly, I say to you, till heaven and earth pass away, one jot or one tittle will by no means pass from the law till all is fulfilled" (Matthew 5:18 NKJV). Just how detailed should we expect that declaration to be?

A *jot* is the smallest letter in the Hebrew alphabet. It looks like a heavy apostrophe as shown by the first letter in the white box.

Jot and Tittle

A *tittle* is a small decorative spur and looks like a little hair coming up out of a letter, like those over the letters in the white box. Five tittles together were called a "crown" and were often used to decorate certain letters.

To emphasize the truth that Scripture is moving within history to accomplish God's purpose, Jesus said that not one of these jots or tittles will disappear. His truth is eternal, and all of his promises to us will be fulfilled.

Look at the smallest letters and the tiniest decorations in these words. See how words have been re-inked to preserve them? Throughout this scroll, you can see how God has protected even the smallest of details in a most astounding way. They are powerful reminders of Jesus' reassuring truth that his Word is eternal and can be counted on.

Moses wrote to tell the children of Israel to "fear the LORD your God and worship him" (Deuteronomy 10:20). To fear God means to be in awe of him, to revere him and worship him as the almighty God who shows mercy and grace to his people. That awesome reverence is clearly evident in the way the scribes performed their solemn duty to pass down the Scriptures from one generation to the next with such precision and accuracy.

Imagine our scribe, Baruch, sitting down to begin his great task of copying the Lodz Torah. If he followed typical Jewish tradition, he would dip his new quill in the freshly prepared ink and speak each word out loud before writing it. As his training had taught him to do, he would pronounce each word correctly and copy each letter exactly. He was even forbidden to touch a letter after it was inked.

"In the beginning," he says aloud as he forms the letters in the first words of the Bible with painstaking precision. But before completing the last letter of the word *beginning*, Baruch stops. The next word in the text is *God*, so, according to the Masoretic scribal tradition, he sets down his quill and ceremoniously washes his hands, purifying himself and sanctifying (setting apart) the ink that will pen the holy name. Only then does he write the word *Elohim* for God.

One of the older traditions of the scribes was that they were not to write the name for God directly after dipping their pens, for fear that the tip of the quill would carry too much ink. The name of God must not be blotted or smudged by excessive ink.

If Baruch followed this tradition, he would select a fresh quill, dip it in the ink, and form the last letter of *beginning* before carefully writing the name of God.

Elohim

He copies each letter in separate, smooth strokes without allowing one letter to touch another. He must be certain to complete the glorious name before lifting his head.

What reverence, what awe, what fear this scribe had in copying God's sacred words. Although writing God's name may have required special ceremonial reverence, every letter Baruch penned was to be exact and never, ever touch another letter. The text of God's Word was truly sacred to Baruch and the other scribes of the Masoretic tradition.

There are twenty-two letters in the Hebrew alphabet. The scribes were given specific instructions for how to form each letter perfectly. For example, the jot or *yud* is the smallest letter in the alphabet.

Jot

The *yud* must have a little leg on the right side and a small tag on its upper left side. The scribe must bend the head of the letter down a little on the left, like a small prickle pointing downward. But the prickle must be shorter than the leg on the right side, lest the *yud* resemble two other Hebrew letters (*resh* and *vav*). If the letter was not formed precisely in this way, it was invalidated and must be erased and penned over. Our Baruch would want each letter to be so clear and perfect that not even a child could misread the smallest one; mistake it for another, similar Hebrew letter; mispronounce it; or misinterpret the meaning of the text.

The Torah was sacred, and the ink was not to be touched by human hands out of the sacredness of the text. The reader in the synagogue must use a pointer to follow the words along the perfectly laid out columns.

You will notice that our scribe occasionally elongated a letter at the end of a word. For example, notice the horizontal line at the end of this word.

These lines had an important function—to slow down the reader long enough to think about the meaning of the sacred text. Not only did the scribes want to copy the Scripture exactly; they also wanted the people to interpret it correctly.

A different technique is used for the same purpose, mostly in the Psalms, where it appears seventy-four times. It is the word *selah*, first used in Psalm 3:4, which the Amplified Bible translates as "pause, and calmly think of that." In other words, "slow down and meditate on this, because it is very important."

The scribe who copied the Lodz Torah also used another technique to get the reader to pause. At times, he would enlarge letters to signify that this passage is very important or that there is a variant reading. This is one characteristic that helps to date the scroll, for it was a writing style used only during medieval times and not before or after. Notice the uniqueness of *this* letter.

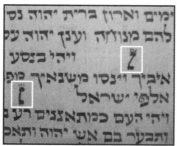

Inverted Nun

It is the fourteenth letter in the Hebrew alphabet, called a *nun*. This is an inverted *nun* adorned with tittles. It was used to indicate that this passage can also be found in another section or should be in another place. It was the scribe's way of telling the reader that the sentence belonged in another section of Scripture, but he was not going to put it there. Why? Because the scribes were careful to copy the Scripture exactly as the earlier manuscript dictated. They were not going to move a sentence to where it might actually belong, because they were committed to replicating the new manuscript exactly as the old one was written. Every time this passage was read, the inverted *nun* served as a reminder of how important the copying of this Torah was to the scribe. It still is to this day.

Dr. Scott Carroll spoke at our Discover the Evidence event where we uncovered the biblical manuscript fragment I had acquired. He made an interesting comment about scribes making errors:

> *I talked to a Jewish scribe friend of mine two weeks ago*
> *in Israel—a sofer. I said, "How many mistakes do you*

make when you transmit?" He's been doing it twenty-five years. He said, "Well, I catch and correct many as I'm writing, but then when I go back through it again, there are probably one hundred that I miss. Then I send it to a friend, and he finds forty more! And then we send it to a computer, and it finds twenty more!"

What does that tell you at the end of the day? Look at all the errors? No! LOOK AT ALL THE CORRECTIONS!

Scribes of the ancient world were human, and they did make mistakes. But because of the extreme care they took in copying God's Word, we can look at all their corrections and know we have an accurate Hebrew text.

Once our scribe, Baruch, completed the last letter of the last word of this Torah, it had to be certified by other scribes or the rabbi. Some traditions required three separate rabbis to check its accuracy. This meant unrolling the seventy-two-foot scroll to check and count every single word and all 304,805 letters. Before a copy could be certified, the scribes and rabbis had to ascertain that it contained precisely the same number of letters as the Torah from which it was copied. Not only that, but when they counted the words, they would indicate the *center word* within the Torah. They knew that the center word was found in Leviticus 13:33. If the center word of the new scroll did not fall exactly within verse 33, that scroll could not be certified.

The scribes counted not only every word, but also every letter. The *center letter* of the Torah was found in Leviticus 11:45. If the new scroll's center letter appeared in verse 45, then the scribes were confident they had an exact replica of the previous Torah.

To certify the new Torah, it was also common to make sure that each word began in the exact same place as in the Torah from which it was copied. If, while copying a given line, a scribe saw that a word that should be retained on that line was about to go to the next, he would compress the letters in order to fit the word onto the line. Yet he couldn't touch one letter against another. Conversely, if he saw he was going to have too much space on a given line, he would stretch letters out in order to make the last letter of the last word align exactly with the left margin. As the scribe copied, each line had to begin and end with the same word and letter as the source Torah, so that the new copy matched the source perfectly. Every precaution was taken to be certain that each new Torah was an exact duplicate of the previous one.

Notice that there are dots on top of some of the letters.

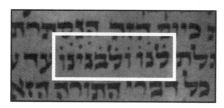

Dots

These are highlighted by the white rectangle in the photograph. There are dots along the top of these letters. These are a way to caution the reader that there might be a textual problem or a different exegesis for this passage. Even so, the scribe could not correct this possible problem by copying it differently. Because he was committed to the exactness of each letter and word, he had to copy it as it was in the older manuscript.

As you can see, God instilled into his scribes a painstaking reverence for the Hebrew Scriptures. When you examine the Lodz Torah, you realize the sacrifice that went into preserving the Word of God—devoted care, obsessive detail, and a sacred reverence in the shaping of each letter and word. These dedicated scribes were intent on producing an exact transmission of the book of the law, so that you and I—and our children—would have an accurate revelation of the God we worship.

Other Common Early Writing Materials

The Lodz Torah was written on calfskin, but calfskin (called *parchment* when treated) was just one of several materials the scribes and other writers used in early times. Other writing materials of the ancient world included

- Clay (Ezekiel 4:1)
- Stone (Exodus 24:12)
- Metal (Exodus 28:36)
- Papyrus (Revelation 5:1)

After calfskin, papyrus was the most commonly used writing material for early manuscripts. *Papyrus* is a Greek term from which we get our English word *paper*. Papyrus was made from the papyrus reed. Those reeds were plentiful in the shallow lakes and rivers of Egypt and Syria.

To prepare papyrus for writing, the reeds were stripped and then cut lengthwise into thin, narrow slices that were then beaten and pressed together into two layers set at right angles to each other. Once dried, they were polished smooth, typically with a stone.

Just as it was typical to sew together manuscript panels made of animal skins to create a scroll, papyrus sheets were also linked into scrolls. This was done by gluing the edges of the sheets together and then winding them around a stick. Papyrus sheets were also pressed together in individual leaf form, like modern books, with writing on both sides, in order to make reading easier and the form less bulky. This was called *codex* or *book* form. It is said that Christianity was the primary reason for the development and spread of the codex, which is the book form we use today.

Prior to the invention of the printing press, anything in writing had to be copied by hand if it was going to be preserved for future generations. As mentioned earlier, no original writings from the Old or New Testaments have been found. Those original writings—from Moses, the prophets, and the apostles—are called the *Autographa*. Once an individual *Autographa* was transcribed into a handwritten copy, it was referred to as a *manuscript*. Eventually, every manuscript would deteriorate, the ink would fade or chip away, and a new manuscript copy would be needed.

Some of the oldest scroll manuscripts made of calfskin date from around 1500 BC.[1] The oldest known papyrus fragments date back to 2400 BC.[2] It was difficult for these earliest papyrus manuscripts to survive, except in dry areas such as the sands of Egypt or in caves.

The real question that arises about the manuscript copies of Scripture relates not so much to their materials and processes, but to their reliability. Yes, the ancient Jewish scribes were painstakingly meticulous, and this gives us confidence in the accuracy of the manuscripts that were passed down. But this alone is not enough for absolute certainty. Because, to date, none of the original writings of Scripture have been discovered, we are left with copies of copies of copies that have been handed down from one generation to another. So how are we to be confident that what we have in today's Bible is what was originally written? Without any assurance that we have an accurate rendering of the God-breathed words originally given to God's spokesmen, we can't be certain that we are reading the actual words that God inspired, can we?

The good news is that we can test the reliability of ancient literature. By applying these tests, we are able to determine the historical accuracy and reliability of a given writing. So what are these tests, and how does the Bible stand up to them? That is the subject of our next four chapters.

Tests for Reliability
of Ancient Literature

There wasn't an empty seat in the classroom. As a guest university lecturer, I stepped to the front of the history class and began with a bold statement: "I believe there is more evidence for the reliability of the New Testament than for any other ten pieces of classical literature put together."

The professor for the class was seated in the far corner of the room. At the conclusion of my opening statement, he began to snicker and groan rather loudly. I figured the best approach was to confront his obvious objection up front.

"Excuse me, Professor," I began. "May I ask what you are snickering about?" He replied without hesitation. "I can't believe you have the audacity to claim in a history class that the New Testament is reliable." He chuckled slightly then added, "That's ridiculous!"

I wasn't taken aback by his confrontational tone or his statement. I had heard it many times before and I was ready for it. I calmly posed a simple question to my skeptical friend: "Tell me, Professor, as a historian, what tests would you apply to a piece of historical writing to determine its accuracy and reliability?"

The entire class turned toward the professor to hear his reply, but he had nothing to say. Amazingly, this university professor of history, who claimed the New Testament was not a reliable historical document, had no means to back up his claim. He had a strong *opinion* that the Bible was unreliable, yet he had no real evidence to support his view.

I explained that there are three basic principles of historiography that pertain to the reliability of literature. Historiography is simply a method of investigation and study of historical events and the way they have been recorded. The principles or tests to determine the reliability of a historical record include the following:

- The *bibliographical* test: determining whether the

text of the historical record has been transmitted accurately.

- The *external evidence* test: determining whether the historical record has been verified or affirmed by data outside itself.
- The *internal evidence* test: determining how the historical record stands up to the test of internal validity.

To determine whether the Bible, or any ancient historical record, is reliable, we must put it to these three tests. Let's examine what these tests require, and then we will put the Bible to the test.

The Bibliographical Test

As we have said before, we don't have an original written document from any of the ancient authors of history—not just of the Bible, but of any historical writing. But that doesn't mean the copies are necessarily unreliable. We do, however, need to ask at least two fundamental questions to evaluate the reliability of a copy:

1. How many manuscript copies of that document have survived?
2. What interval of time elapsed between the original writing and the earliest existing copy?

This bibliographical test assesses the trustworthiness of any work of literature based on the wise supposition that the more copies we can gather of a work—and the nearer in time those copies are to the original—the greater our certainty that we possess the text as originally written. The more copies we have of an original writing, the better we can compare one to another to see if they are consistent. Ideally, they will be close replicas of each other. And it stands to reason that the earliest copy made from the original would be the most trustworthy. The more removed a copy is from the original, the greater the chances that any copying mistakes would be replicated in subsequent copies.

To give us a basis for comparison of how the Bible holds up under the bibliographical test, it is useful to consider how other ancient documents fare. As we have indicated, every work of ancient literature (that is, anything produced before the invention of the printing press) had to be copied repeatedly throughout the centuries to preserve it from loss through decay. But copies of classic works are often incomplete. They contain errors—slips of the pen, missing segments, misspelled words, and so on. These errors, of course, are passed down through generations of copying. And this is why having multiple copies available greatly helps scholars who want to cross-check manuscripts. And again, the older the copies the better.

Surprisingly few copies of many ancient writings still exist today. Some are still being discovered by the same process through which I acquired the New Testament fragments. Still, many modern editions of ancient books are based on a mere handful of copies (or maybe as many as a few hundred), all of which were created centuries after the original composition. Take the historical record of Caesar's *Gallic Wars* for example. The wars themselves lasted from 58 BC to 50 BC, and the last of the books was composed no later than 44 BC. For years scholars reported there were only ten of these manuscripts in existence. Today, just over 250 such manuscripts (and counting) have been found, the earliest of which was copied in the ninth century AD, and the majority are from the fifteenth century. This means the oldest copy was made some 950 years after Caesar's wars.

With these ancient records, scholars were able to piece together Caesar's exploits and battle strategy, which made the books very influential in Europe centuries after they were written. During the

1500s, for example, the Holy Roman Emperor Charles V studied the documents to gain insight into battle strategy.[1]

By 1468, not long after the printing press was invented in Europe, *Gallic Wars* was considered a classic and was published in Rome.[2] In 1972, all the extant manuscripts of the work, including the textual background of each manuscript, were catalogued and published by Brill Academic Publishers in the Netherlands.[3] The point is that Caesar's *Gallic Wars* is considered to pass the bibliographical test for being a reliable and accurate historical record, with just over 250 manuscripts in existence and 950 years between the original writing and the earliest existing copy.

Copies of other ancient works of history pass the bibliographical test with even less manuscript evidence. The modern text of Livy's *History of Rome*, for example, is based on ninety early-fifth-century manuscripts and sixty much later copies that are dated from four hundred to one thousand years after the original writing.[4]

The History of the Peloponnesian War, by Thucydides, who lived sometime between 460 BC and 400 BC, is based primarily on numerous papyrus fragments from the early Christian era and eight complete manuscripts, the earliest from around AD 900. The manuscripts of *The Histories of Herodotus*, by the ancient Greek historian, boast forty-nine papyrus fragments and some parchment manuscripts from the first century AD.[5] The late F. F. Bruce, at one time the Ryland Professor of Biblical Criticism at the University of Manchester, England, defends the reliability of these works: "No classical scholar would listen to an argument that the authenticity of Herodotus or Thucydides is in doubt because the earliest manuscripts of their works which are of use to us are over 1,300 years later than the originals."[6]

Even working with scant evidence from these ancient documents, scholars can be confident they have met the first test in determining the authenticity and correct reading of the original documents.

The External Evidence Test

The second test to help scholars evaluate an ancient writing's reliability is the external evidence test, which determines whether other historical materials confirm or conflict with the internal testimony of the document itself. In other words, can writings be found apart from the literature under analysis that substantiate its accuracy, reliability, and authenticity?

For example, another ancient author may quote passages from Caesar's *Gallic Wars* or make reference to the occurrence of a particular war. This external evidence would support our belief that the events in question actually took place, and it would lend credibility to the document under investigation.

Another form of corroborating external evidence would be physical artifacts that somehow support the ancient writing. Let's say that unique armaments were found dating back to Caesar's time that matched the description in the *Gallic Wars* documents. Or perhaps human bones or weapons were uncovered on a battlefield documented in the work. This would further attest to the reliability of the historical record. There have been many finds through recent archaeological discoveries that reinforce numerous ancient writings. Simply stated, when evidence outside the writing in question is confirmed, it bolsters the reliability of that writing.

The Internal Evidence Test

The third test—internal evidence—weighs whether a book is consistent within itself and whether the authors can be trusted to tell the truth. Is the book filled with contradictions? Is there evidence that the bias of the writers caused them to lose objectivity and distort the facts? There are generally three standards used to answer these questions and test the internal reliability of a historical document.

1. Give the Text the Benefit of the Doubt

We all can recall instances when we felt treated unfairly by an authority figure—a teacher or boss or parent. The person prejudged us and decided that no matter what we did, it was wrong. We were judged guilty until proven innocent.

Some critics develop that same unfair attitude toward certain books, and often toward the Bible. They come to the book with a prejudice against the possibility of miracles, for example; or, like the history professor I encountered above, with a resistance to the Bible's claim to be authoritative. They treat unexplained details as errors and find discrepancies where none exist.

Yet an objective reader must approach any book—Scripture included—with openness to the statements of the author. Disliking or having difficulty with a doctrine, a fact of history, or a truth claim does not necessarily mean it should be regarded as untrue.

Whether evaluating the Bible or any other book, we have an obligation simply to be fair. If the text of a book is "innocent until proven guilty," the burden of proof is on the critic to show that a difficulty within the writing constitutes a real error.

2. Freedom from Known Contradiction

Let's say that somewhere in two of the manuscripts of Caesar's *Gallic Wars* the text states that Caesar never married. Yet it was widely known and historically documented elsewhere that Caesar's first wife was Cornelia, daughter of Lucius Cornelius Cinna. Further, what if other manuscripts of the *Gallic Wars* cited a woman by the name of Aurelia as Caesar's first wife? Those contradictions would be problematic, and if they could not be reconciled, the entire record might be called into question.

In evaluating any ancient manuscript, objective scholars apply a principle that any alleged contradictions in the work must be demonstrated to be impossible to reconcile, not merely difficult to reconcile. Scholar and author Robert M. Horn describes the conditions that must be met in order to demonstrate that a text contains genuine mistakes. Far more is required, he says, than "the mere appearance of a contradiction." First, we must be certain we have understood a passage properly—how it uses words and numbers, for example. Second, we must know all that can be reasonably known about the subject treated in the text. And third, we must be sure that new discoveries in textual research, archaeology, and so on couldn't possibly shed more light on the passage. Horn concludes:

> *Difficulties do not constitute objections. Unsolved problems are not of necessity errors. This is not to minimize the area of difficulty; it is to see it in perspective. Difficulties are to be grappled with and problems are to drive us to seek clearer light; but until such time as we have total and final light on any issue, we are in no position to affirm, "Here is a proven error or an unquestionable objection."[7]*

3. The Use of Primary Sources

Candidates for public office and recently elected officials in the United States have been known to resign or drop out of a race when certain of their writings or speeches were found to be plagiarized. Newspaper reporters have occasionally been caught inventing sources and fabricating information to pump up their stories. These inappropriate methods of reporting a story, however, are not new.

A survey of ancient writings shows that many writers adhered only loosely to the facts of the events they reported. Some highly regarded authors of the ancient world reported events that took place many years before they were born and in countries they had never visited. Though their writing may be largely factual, historians admit that greater credibility must be granted to writers who were both geographically and chronologically close to the events they report.

How Does the Bible Hold Up under These Tests?

My friend the history professor found my statement about the reliability of the New Testament to be ridiculous. There are a lot of critics who claim that the Old and New Testaments are inaccurate and unreliable. Some, for example, claim that Moses could not have written the first five books of the Bible because writing did not exist in Moses' day. Others assert that the New Testament was not written until late in the second century AD. And then what was written was composed from mere myths and legends. They conclude that there is no credibility at all to the New Testament. A little over ten years ago, a popular event added fuel to this incredulity. It was the publication of a successful novel by author Dan Brown, followed by a blockbuster movie based on the book. In his thriller titled *The DaVinci Code*, Brown claims that "more than eighty gospels were considered for the New Testament, and yet only a relative few were chosen for inclusion."[8] Because of this claim, many people began to question the reliability of the Gospels.

There are many such critics and outlandish claims that attempt to discredit the Bible. But are they accurate? Do they have a point? Or when we put Scripture to the test, do we find that it is a truly reliable document of history? Don't take my word for it; let's journey together in the next three chapters and apply the three tests of historical reliability to the Bible.

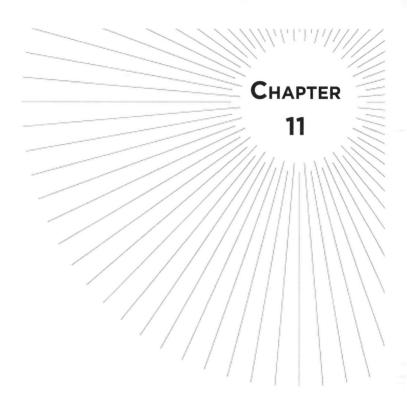
Testing the Historical Reliability of the Old Testament

If the Old Testament is God-breathed words, as we believe it is; if God has supernaturally superintended its transmission down through the ages, as we believe he has; then the Old Testament should have no problem standing up to the three tests of reliability: the bibliographical test, the internal evidence test, and the external evidence test. So how does the Hebrew text stack up?

Bibliographical Test

We have made reference to a number of ancient manuscripts, such as Caesar's *Gallic Wars*, Livy's *History of Rome*, Thucydides's *History of the Peloponnesian War*, and *The Histories of Herodotus*, all of which were written between 480 BC and AD 17. These documents boast anywhere from a handful of manuscripts to just over 250 in existence today. But the evidence supporting those manuscripts pales in comparison to one of the most recognized and historically reliable works, which is Homer's *Iliad* (800 BC). There are more than 1,800 *Iliad* manuscripts in existence, and the earliest manuscript copy dates to 400 BC.[1] But the *Iliad* can't come even close to the number of Old Testament manuscript fragments and scrolls that have been found. Here is a brief survey of the most significant finds of ancient Hebrew texts.

In the late nineteenth century, almost 250,000 Jewish manuscript fragments of the Old Testament were found in the genizah (a storeroom or cabinet for old manuscripts) of the Ben Ezra Synagogue in Old Cairo. Those documents were written from about AD 870 to AD 1880.[2] A few years ago, more than 24,000 biblical-related materials were published from this Cairo Genizah Collection.[3]

A medieval bound Hebrew manuscript called the Aleppo Codex was copied in about AD 925. Remember that *codex* is the term used for a book made up of sheets of leather (parchment or vellum) rather than linked in scroll form. Many scholars consider the Aleppo Codex to be the most authoritative copy of the Masoretic text. Originally copied as a complete Hebrew text (Old Testament), only 294 of the original 487 manuscript pages survive today.[4]

The Leningrad Codex (AD 1008), a complete copy of the entire Hebrew text, is housed in the National Library of Russia. Practically all modern English translations of the Old Testament are based on the Leningrad Codex.[5]

By the 1940s, thousands of Old Testament manuscript fragments, along with dozens of scrolls, had been discovered. But this was only the beginning.

In the spring of 1947, a young Bedouin shepherd made the greatest manuscript discovery of all time. As author Ralph Earle summarizes the story in his book *How We Got Our Bible*, the shepherd boy "tossed a stone into a hole in a cliff on the west side of the Dead Sea, about eight miles south of Jericho near an ancient site called Qumran. To his surprise, he heard the sound of shattering pottery. Investigating, he discovered an amazing sight. On the floor of the cave were several large jars containing leather scrolls, wrapped in linen cloth."[6]

Once archaeologists completed their search of the Qumran caves—eleven caves in all—almost 1,050 scrolls had been found in about 25,000 to 50,000 pieces (a number that varies depending on how the fragments are counted).[7] Of these manuscripts, about three hundred were texts from the Bible, and many of the rest had "direct relevance to early Judaism and emerging Christianity."[8] Every book of the Old Testament was represented, except for the book of Esther, and the earliest copies dated from about 250 BC.

With the discovery of the Dead Sea Scrolls, as the Qumran manuscripts are commonly known, we now have Old Testament texts 1,175 years older than the very reliable Aleppo Codex. We can also compare the Leningrad Codex to the Dead Sea Scrolls, which are 1,258 years older.

Now here's the exciting part: Once the Dead Sea Scrolls were translated and compared with modern versions of the Hebrew Bible, the text proved to be identical, word for word, in more than 95 percent of the cases. (The 5 percent deviation consists mainly of spelling variations. For example, of the 166 words in Isaiah 53, only seventeen letters are in question. Of those, ten are a matter of spelling, and four are stylistic differences; the remaining three letters comprise the word *light*, which was added to Isaiah 53:11.)[9]

In other words, the greatest manuscript discovery of all time revealed that more than one thousand years of copying the Old Testament had produced only very minor variations, none of which altered the clear meaning of the text or brought the manuscript's fundamental integrity into question.

Dr. Peter Flint spoke at the Discover the Evidence event where we uncovered the biblical manuscript fragments I had acquired. He is the director of the Dead Sea Scrolls Institute at Trinity Western University in British Columbia and author of a book titled *The Dead Sea Scrolls*, which I have used as a source. Dr. Flint has firsthand knowledge of the Dead Sea Scrolls because he edited or coedited almost thirty of the scrolls for publication. Here is what he said, in part, at the event about how the scrolls confirm the later Hebrew text:

> *The biblical Dead Sea Scrolls are up to 1,250 years older than the traditional Hebrew Bible, the Masoretic text. We had been using a one-thousand-year-old manuscript to make our Bibles. We've now got scrolls going back to 250 BC.*
>
> *So now here is the million-dollar question. When we take the biblical scrolls and we compare them with our Hebrew Bible, what do we get? Maybe you've had this experience. Someone has visited you at your doorstep and said to you, "Your Bible is full of errors. The church has messed with it and your Bible's been changed." Now we*

can take our current Bible and compare it with the Dead Sea Scrolls to see if it has changed. When our Bible is compared with the biblical scrolls, what is our conclusion? Our conclusion is simply this—the scrolls confirm the accuracy of the biblical text by 99 percent.

Let's give an example of a very famous passage from Psalm 22: "My God, my God, why have you forsaken me?" This is the psalm that Jesus cried on the cross. In the Gospels, the writer relates this passage to the crucifixion. In the King James, it renders Psalm 22:16 like this: "Dogs have surrounded me, a pack of evil ones close in on me; they have pierced my hands and my feet."

Now, you know this verse and you would say, "This is the prophecy of Christ's crucifixion." Did you know that, in fact, if you took this verse and spoke to a rabbi or even a Bible scholar, they would say, "Not so fast." Because if you turn to the Hebrew Bible that was translated from the Leningrad Codex, you would be quite shocked to discover it doesn't say that. The Leningrad Codex says, "Dogs surround me, a pack of evil ones close in on me like a lion on my hands and feet."

Now some would say, "You see, the church has messed with the text. They wanted to put Jesus in their text, so they ignored the Hebrew wording and put in 'they've pierced my hands and feet.' " That is a great challenge, but, my friends, I've got good news for you. This passage is preserved in one of the Dead Sea Scrolls, and I know what I'm talking about because I am the editor of that scroll. It contains this passage. It is in the oldest copy of Psalm 22 in the world and it says: "Dogs have surrounded me, a band of evil ones have encircled me; they have pierced my hands and my feet." Isn't that amazing?

It *is* amazing. And because the earliest manuscript is given the greater authority, the rendering used by the King James translators ends up being the correct one. It also makes sense that, if the original autographs are God-breathed words, then God would miraculously superintend the Scripture so it is passed down accurately to us.

When all the manuscripts of the Old Testament are tallied, how many are in existence today? The traditional listings of Old Testament manuscripts normally leave out the abundant scroll evidence. New finds are happening constantly, so it is not easy to determine an exact number of hand-copied Old Testament manuscripts.

After conferring with experts such as Dr. Scott Carroll, Dr. Peter Flint, Father Columba Stewart, executive director of the Hill Museum and Manuscript Library at Saint John's University in Collegeville, Minnesota, and others, I've estimated that at least seventeen thousand Hebrew scrolls and codices, dated earlier than the eighteenth century, exist today.[10] The manuscript authority of Homer's *Iliad*, with more than eighteen hundred manuscripts in existence, is truly impressive. By comparison, the Old Testament manuscript authority of some seventeen thousand manuscripts is beyond impressive.

Calculating the time between the original writings of the Old Testament and the earliest existing copies depends on which of its thirty-nine books is under review. We're not certain of the exact dates of Moses' writings, for example. If he wrote the Pentateuch in the latter years of his life, the time interval between the writing of the first five books of the Old Testament and the earliest Dead Sea Scroll copy would be about 1,100 years.[11] The other thirty-four books of the Old Testament were written later, some as late as 460 BC, making the time interval between the originals and the existing manuscripts of the Dead Sea Scrolls much shorter.

When we analyze how the scribes meticulously copied the Hebrew text, and then consider the number of manuscripts in existence and the time interval between the original writing and the earliest existing copies, the Old Testament more than meets the bibliographical test—without question! By this standard, the Old Testament we have today is truly historically reliable.

External Evidence Test

When determining the reliability of any ancient writing, historians will ask, "Which sources, apart from the literature under examination, substantiate its accuracy and reliability?" Without question, the Bible is the most widely referenced and quoted book of all time.

In addition to extrabiblical references, the Bible—the Old Testament in particular—has been regularly and consistently supported by archaeology. Until the late eighteenth century, the pursuit of biblical relics in the Near East was the work of amateur treasure hunters, whose methods included grave robbing. The discovery of the Rosetta Stone in Egypt by Napoleon's army in 1799 changed everything. Biblical archaeology became the domain of respected archaeologists. The excavation of ancient ruins all across the Near East has shed new light on peoples and events mentioned in Scripture.

Archaeology has established the historicity of the people and events described in the Bible, yielding more than twenty-five thousand finds that either directly or indirectly relate to Scripture. Moreover, the historical existence of some thirty individuals named in the New Testament, and nearly sixty from the Old Testament, has been confirmed through archaeological and historical research. Only a small fraction of possible biblical sites have been excavated in the Holy Land, and much more could be published on existing excavations. Even so, the external evidence of archaeological data we now possess clearly indicates that the Old Testament is historically reliable and not the product of myth, superstition, or embellishment.

You can find a wealth of information on archaeological discoveries related to both the New and Old Testaments in study Bibles—such as the *Apologetics Study Bible for Students* published by Holman Bible Publishers, under the section titled "Bones and Dirt Notes." In my own book *The New Evidence That Demands a Verdict*, I devote a substantial section to archaeology of the Old Testament, and an entire chapter to the subject of archaeology and biblical criticism.[12]

Below we'll look at some examples of how archaeology provides external evidence that the historical record of the Old Testament is reliable.

The Existence of Babylon and King Nebuchadnezzar

The book of Daniel refers to the great city of Babylon and a king known as Nebuchadnezzar, who was said to have lived and reigned over Babylon from 605 BC to 565 BC. Yet for many years, critics claimed that such a city and king never existed. But now his existence has been irrefutably confirmed by archaeologists who uncovered evidence near present-day Hillah, Babylon Province, Iraq, about fifty-five miles south of Baghdad.

Numerous fragments of bricks with remains of white-glazed cuneiform characters have been found that belong to a building inscription of Nebuchadnezzar II at the Ishtar Gate of Babylon. Archaeologists claim there is no doubt that the text refers to the construction of the gate. The text was restored by comparison with another complete inscription found on a limestone block that gives three excerpts of the main inscription of the king stating: "I, Nebuchadnezzar, laid the foundation of the gates. . . . I magnificently adorned them with luxurious splendor for all mankind to behold in awe."[13]

The Tower of Babel

The book of Genesis records a time when everyone spoke one language and the people set out to build a tower that reached high into the sky—the famed Tower of Babel story often recounted in Sunday school. Critics have scoffed at the story and claimed that no such event ever happened.

However, Sumerian literature refers to a time in history when there was a single language. Archaeology has also uncovered evidence that Ur-Nammu, king of Ur from about 2044 BC to 2007 BC, built a great *ziggurat* (temple tower) as an act of worship to the moon god Nanna. A *stele* (monument) about five feet across and ten feet high reveals Ur-Nammu's activities. One artifact panel shows the king setting out with a mortar basket to begin construction of the great tower, thus showing his allegiance to the gods as he takes his place as a humble workman.[14]

Another clay tablet states that the erection of the tower offended the gods, so they threw down what the men had built, scattered them abroad, and made their speech strange. These descriptions are remarkably similar to the Genesis account of the Tower of Babel.

Sodom and Gomorrah

The destruction of Sodom and Gomorrah was regarded as religious legend until evidence revealed that all five of the cities mentioned as allies of Sodom in Genesis 14 were in fact centers of commerce in the area and were geographically situated as the Scriptures describe. The biblical description of their destruction appears to be just as accurate. Geological evidence in the area points to ancient earthquake activity disrupting the layers of the earth and hurling them high into the air. In addition, the evidence indicates that the present layers of sedimentary rock were melded together by intense heat, pointing to a great conflagration, possibly when an oil basin beneath the Dead Sea ignited and erupted. Bitumen is plentiful on the site, and an accurate description of the event would be that brimstone (bituminous pitch) was hurled up into the air by the force of the eruption and rained down on those cities.[15]

Balaam Inscription

The story of Balaam and his talking donkey (Numbers 22:22–40) was viewed skeptically by critical scholars for many decades. It was even doubted that Balaam ever existed. This outlook began to change in 1967 when archaeologists collected a crumbled plaster Aramaic text in the rubble of an ancient building in Deir 'Alla (Jordan). The text contains fifty lines written in faded red and black ink. The inscription reads: "Warnings from the Book of Balaam the son of Beor. He was a seer of the gods." This corresponds exactly to what we read in Numbers 22:5 and Joshua 24:9. Though the building in which the text was found dates back only to the eighth century BC (during the reign of Judah's King Uzziah; see Isaiah 6:1), the condition of the plaster and the ink of the text itself indicates that it is most likely much older, dating to the time of the biblical Balaam.

In addition to Balaam, nearly sixty other Old Testament figures have been either historically or archaeologically identified. These include kings David (1 Samuel 16:13), Jehu (2 Kings 9:2), Omri (1 Kings 16:22), Uzziah (Isaiah 6:1), Jotham (2 Kings 15:7), Hezekiah (Isaiah 37:1), Jehoiachin (2 Chronicles 36:8) , Shalmaneser V (2 Kings 17:3), Tiglath-pileser III (1 Chronicles 5:6), Sargon II (Isaiah 20:1), Sennacherib (Isaiah 36:1), Nebuchadnezzar (Daniel 2:1), Belshazzar (Daniel 5:1), Cyrus (Isaiah 45:1), and others.[16]

Ebla Tablets

Critics have long scoffed at the idea that certain ancient cities with commerce, advanced social structure, and forms of writing could have existed when the Hebrew text claimed Israel came into being. The common view was that such an advanced civilization could not have arisen until the 800s BC.

Then, in 1976, an Italian archaeologist named Paolo Matthiae discovered the Ebla Tablets at Tell Mardikh in Aleppo, Syria. These tablets represent a royal archive of more than sixteen thousand clay tablets dating from 2400 BC. They provide a glimpse into the lifestyle, vocabulary, commerce, geography, and religion of the peoples who lived near Canaan (later called Israel) in the time immediately before Abraham, Isaac, and Jacob. Translations of several tablets by Giovanni Pettinato, in his *Archives of Ebla: An Empire Inscribed in Clay*, support the existence of biblical cities such as Sodom (Genesis 19:1), Zeboiim (Genesis 14:2, 8), Admah (Genesis 10:19), Hazor (1 Kings 9:15), Megiddo (1 Chronicles 7:29), Canaan (Genesis 48:3), and Jerusalem (Jeremiah 1:15).

Further, the tablets include personal names likened to biblical persons such as Nahor (Genesis 11:22–25), Israel (Genesis 32:28), Eber (Genesis 10:21–25), Michael (Numbers 13:13), and Ishmael (Genesis 16:11). Regarding vocabulary, the tablets contain certain words similar to those used in the Bible, such as *tehom*, which in Genesis 1:2 is translated as "the deep." The tablets also provide information related to Hebrew literary style and religion, helping us to understand the civilizations in the region that became known as Israel.[17]

In this chapter, we have subjected the Old Testament Scriptures to two of the tests routinely applied to determine the reliability of ancient texts—the bibliographical test and the external evidence test. As we can see, the reliability of the Old Testament has been confirmed repeatedly throughout history. The next test is the internal evidence test. But before we delve into that test, I want to apply the bibliographical and external evidence tests to the New Testament, which we will do in the next chapter. Then, in chapter 13, we will apply the internal evidence test to both the Old and New Testaments. This approach will allow us adequate space to address the alleged internal contradictions in the Bible often cited by critics.

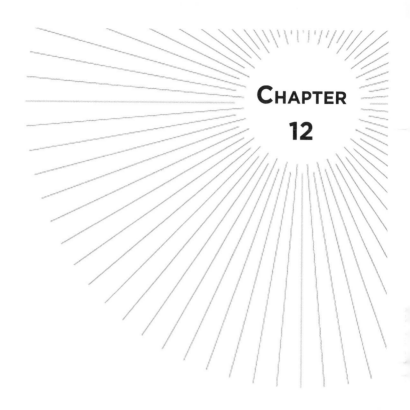

Testing the Historical Reliability of the New Testament

By the time this book is published, the statistics I've cited for the number of Old Testament manuscripts in existence, and the numbers I'm about to give concerning New Testament manuscripts, will all be out of date. That's because biblical archaeology is an ongoing pursuit and scientists are continually making new discoveries. Dr. Scott Carroll made the following statement at the Discover the Evidence seminar in December 2013: "Working with other scholars around the world, major New Testament and Old Testament discoveries have been made. . .and they're being made on an ongoing basis. Literally, every week!"

Some of these new discoveries, like the New and Old Testament fragments I acquired in 2013, are some of the earliest known manuscript passages in existence. Each time we discover more fragments such as these, they add to the already massive numbers of Old and New Testament manuscripts and give us new opportunities for comparison to other copies. This is also true of other ancient works, such as the writings of Plato, Homer, Caesar, and others.

In the past ten years alone, more than 1,100 additional manuscript fragments of Homer's *Iliad* have been discovered, more than 240 manuscript portions of Caesar's *Gallic Wars* have been found, and more than 200 of Plato's Tetralogies (four-part arrangements of Plato's dialogues) have been added to the list, along with many other examples of ancient literature. Each new discovery elevates the reliability of the text for each document, according to the bibliographical test.

Bibliographical Test

The manuscript authority of the twenty-seven books of the New Testament is exemplary, both in terms of sheer numbers and in the time intervals between the original autographs and the earliest existing copies. Today, there are more than twenty-four thousand New Testament manuscripts in libraries, universities, and private collections throughout the world. The earliest of these is a fragment of the Gospel of John currently located in the John Rylands Library in Manchester, England. It has been dated to within fifty years of the time when the apostle John penned the original.[1]

Following is a chart listing nine ancient classical writings, along with their authors, dates of the original writing and the earliest discovered manuscripts, the time gaps in years, and the number of manuscripts in existence at the present time. The chart also lists the number of manuscripts extant just ten years ago. Using the bibliographical test, we can compare the data from these classics with that of the New Testament. As you will see, the comparative differences are quite remarkable.

A COMPARISON OF ANCIENT WORKS WITH THE NEW TESTAMENT[2]

Author	Work	Date Written By or Between	Earliest MSS	Time Gap in Years (approx.)	Old #s	New #s
Homer	*Iliad*	800 BC	c. 400 BC	400	643	1,800+
Herodotus	*Histories*	480–425 BC	AD 900	1,350	8	109
Plato	Tetralogies	400 BC	AD 895	1,300	7	210
Caesar	*Gallic Wars*	58–44 BC	AD 900	950	10	250+
Livy	*History of Rome*	59 BC— AD 17	Early 5th century AD (mostly 10th century AD)	400+ (1,000)	1 partial 19 full	90 & 60 copies
Tacitus	*Annals*	AD 100	1st half: AD 850; 2nd half: AD 1050	750–950	20	2 & 31
Pliny, the Elder	*Natural History*	AD 49–79	1 frag. from 5th century; rest 14th–15th century AD	460 (1,450+)	7	200

Author	Work	Date Written By or Between	Earliest MSS	Time Gap in Years (approx.)	Old #s	New #s
Thucydides	*History of Peloponnesian War*	460–400 BC	3rd century BC and AD 900	200 (1,350)	8	96
Demosthenes	Speeches	300 BC	Some frags. from 1st century BC; rest AD 1100	200 (1,400)	200	340
	New Testament	AD 50–100	AD 130 (or earlier)	50+	5,366	5,838
	Greek NT, early translations		AD 400–500	300–400		18,520+

According to the bibliographical test for evaluating the textual reliability of ancient writings, the New Testament impressively passes the test. We have more than thirteen times as many New Testament manuscripts in existence today than we have for Homer's *Iliad*. And when we compare the time gap between the original writings and the earliest existing manuscripts, the New Testament more than passes the test in this area as well. Among documents from the ancient world, the New Testament simply has no equal when it comes to manuscript authority.

External Evidence Test

Since the time of its first composition, the New Testament has been by far the most widely referenced and quoted book in all of history. Leaders, writers, and theologians in the early church often quoted extensive passages from the Gospels and the Epistles. Though some of these quotations are not word for word, they nonetheless serve an indispensable role as external evidence of the content of Scripture.[3] As theologians Norman Geisler and William Nix explain:

> *The writings of the most authoritative writers of the early church—the leaders scholars refer to collectively as the Apostolic Fathers—give overwhelming support to the existence of the twenty-seven authoritative books of the New Testament. Some Apostolic Fathers produced extensive, highly accurate quotes from the text of the New Testament. . . . Early Christian writers provide quotations so numerous and widespread that if no manuscripts of the New Testament were extant, "the New Testament could be reproduced from the writings of the early Fathers alone."* [4]

Geisler and Nix tell us that "there were some 32,000 citations of the New Testament prior to the time of the Council of Nicea (AD 325). These 32,000 quotations are by no means exhaustive, and they do not even include the fourth-century writers. Just adding the number of references used by one other writer, Eusebius, who flourished prior to and contemporary with the Council at Nicea, brings the total number of citations of the New Testament to over 36,000."[5] See the chart below to see how the numbers add up.

EARLY CITATIONS OF THE NEW TESTAMENT

Writer	Gospels	Acts	Pauline Epistles	General Epistles	Revelation	Totals
Justin Martyr	268	10	43	6	3	330
Irenaeus	1,038	194	499	23	65	1,819
Clement of Alexandria	1,017	44	1,127	207	11	2,406

Writer	Gospels	Acts	Pauline Epistles	General Epistles	Revelation	Totals
Origen	9,231	349	7,778	399	165	17,922
Tertullian	3,822	502	2,609	120	205	7,258
Hippolytus	734	42	387	27	188	1,378
Eusebius	3,258	211	1,592	88	27	5,176
Grand Totals	**19,368**	**1,352**	**14,035**	**870**	**664**	**36,289**

Besides verifying the text of the New Testament, early Christian writers also give glimpses of the remarkable care taken in the writing of the biblical accounts of Christ.

- **Eusebius** records comments that can be traced back to the apostle John via the writings of Papias, bishop of Hierapolis (AD 130). Papias reports John's assertion that Mark "wrote down accurately all that he [Peter] mentioned, whether sayings or doings of Christ." And "Mark made no mistake writing down in this way some things as he [Peter] mentioned them; for he paid attention to this one thing, not to omit anything that he had heard, not to include any false statement among them."[6]
- **Irenaeus**, bishop of Lyons, had been a Christian for eighty-six years when he was martyred in AD 156. As a disciple of John's, he was in an excellent position to verify the accounts of Jesus:

> *Matthew published his Gospel among the Hebrews in their own tongue, when Peter and Paul were preaching the gospel in Rome and founding the*

church there. After their departure (i.e., their death,
which strong tradition places at the time of the
Neronian persecution in AD 64), Mark, the disciple
and interpreter of Peter, himself handed down to us
in writing the substance of Peter's preaching. Luke,
the follower of Paul, set down in a book the gospel
preached by his teacher. Then John, the disciple of the
Lord, who also leaned on His breast (this is a reference
to John 13:25 and 21:20), himself produced his
Gospel, while he was living at Ephesus in Asia.[7]

Not only do these early quotations give evidence of the existence of the original New Testament documents, but their consistency corroborated the content of those documents.

In addition to the Christian writers of the first and second century who verified the writings of the New Testament, many non-Christian writers did as well. They confirmed the people, places, and events recorded in the New Testament. Here are a few examples:

• **Tacitus,** a first-century Roman, is considered one of the most accurate historians of the ancient world. He makes references to "Pontius Pilatus, and a most mischievous superstition."[8] "Mischievous superstition" is considered to be his term for the resurrection of Christ.

• **Suetonius** was chief secretary to Emperor Hadrian, who reigned in Rome from AD 117 to 138. He confirms the report in Acts 18:2 that Claudius commanded all Jews to leave Rome in AD 49.[9]

• **Josephus** (AD 37–100) was a Pharisee of the priestly line and a Jewish historian. His writings contain many statements that verify the historical nature of both the Old and New Testaments. Josephus refers to Jesus as the brother of James who was martyred. He writes that Ananias the high priest "assembled the Sanhedrin of the judges, and brought before them the brother of Jesus, who was called Christ, whose name was James, and some others, and when he had formed an accusation against them as breakers of the law, he delivered them to be stoned."[10] This passage, written in AD 93, provides a first-century corroboration of the New Testament reports that Jesus was a real person, that he was identified by others as the Christ, and that he had a brother named James who died a martyr's death at the hands of the high priest and the Sanhedrin.

• **Pliny the Younger** was a Roman author and administrator with access to official information not available to the public. In a letter to Emperor Trajan in about AD 112, Pliny describes the early Christian worship practices:

They were in the habit of meeting on a certain fixed day before it was light, when they sang in alternate verses a hymn to Christ, as to a god, and bound themselves by a solemn oath, not to do any wicked deeds, but never to commit any fraud, theft or adultery, never to falsify their word, nor deny a trust when they should be called upon to deliver it up; after which it was their custom to separate, and then reassemble to partake of food—but food of an ordinary and innocent kind.[11]

> This reference provides solid evidence that Jesus
> Christ was worshipped as God from an early date by
> Christians who continued to follow the practice of
> breaking bread together, as reported in Acts 2:42, 46.

These and many other outside sources give far more substantiation of the reliability of the biblical record than can be found for any other book in ancient history. In addition to these non-Christian writers who verify the New Testament record, there is also corroborating evidence from archaeology.

Archaeologists underscored the reliability of the New Testament in a significant way when they confirmed the absolute accuracy of Luke's accounts in his Gospel and the book of Acts. At one time, critics had concluded that Luke's facts in his detailed report of the birth of Jesus (Luke 2:1–3) were badly garbled: that there was no census; that Quirinius was not governor of Syria at that time; and that citizens were not required to return to their ancestral homes to be counted.[12]

But subsequent archaeological discoveries confirmed Luke's version of the story. First, they showed that the Romans did have a regular enrollment of taxpayers and conducted censuses every fourteen years. This procedure was indeed begun under Augustus, and the first one occurred in either 23–22 BC or 9–8 BC. The latter instance would be the one to which Luke refers. Second, an inscription found in Antioch confirms that Quirinius was governor of Syria around 7 BC.[13] Third, a papyrus found in Egypt gives directions for the conduct of a Roman census. It reads, "Because of the approaching census, it is necessary that all those residing for any cause away from their homes should at once prepare to return to their own governments in order that they may complete the family registration of the enrollment and that the tilled lands may retain those belonging to them."[14]

Research has also laid to rest all doubts about Luke's accuracy in geography, language, and culture. Archaeologists once believed he was completely wrong in placing the cities of Lystra and Derbe in Lycaonia, and Iconium elsewhere (Acts 14:6, 19). The writings of the Roman Cicero contradicted Luke's account, indicating that Iconium was in Lycaonia, Trusting Cicero rather than Luke, archaeologists concluded that the book of Acts was unreliable. However, in 1910, British archaeologist Sir William Ramsay found a monument showing that Iconium was a Phrygian city, a discovery later confirmed by other finds.[15] Many additional archaeological discoveries have identified most of the ancient cities mentioned in the book of Acts. As a result, the journeys of Paul can now be accurately traced.[16]

Linguists also doubted Luke's usage of certain words. A classic case is his reference to the civil authorities in Thessalonica as *politarchs* (Acts 17:6). Since the word *politarch* isn't found in classical literature, Luke was again assumed to be wrong. However, some nineteen inscriptions containing the title have since been found.[17]

Historians questioned Luke's account of the riot in Ephesus, where he describes the event as a civic assembly (Ecclesia) in an amphitheater (Acts 19:23–29). But Luke was again proved right when an inscription was found telling of silver statues of Artemis to be placed in the "theater during a full session of the *Ecclesia*." The theater, when excavated, proved to have room for twenty-five thousand people.[18]

When Jesus talked with his disciples on the Mount of Olives about the building of the temple, he said, "Do you see all these things? . . . Truly I tell you, not one stone here will be left on another; every one will be thrown down" (Matthew 24:2 NIV). The accuracy of Jesus' prophecy is demonstrated by the Arch of Titus, which was constructed as a victory memorial for Emperor Titus (AD 79–81) by his younger brother Emperor Domitian (AD 81–96). Located in Rome between the ancient Forum and the Coliseum, the marble arch depicts the transportation of spoils (the menorah and sacred trumpets) from the ransacked Jerusalem temple.

In addition to this important evidence, more recent excavations in the area of the lower street along the southwest corner of the Jerusalem Temple Mount revealed large stones that had been toppled from the heights by the Romans in their military campaign of AD 70. Today, not one of the original building structures remains standing on the Temple Mount. The depictions and inscription on the Arch of Titus, as well as the rubble found at the Temple Mount in Jerusalem, provide historical verification for the fulfillment of Jesus' prediction that the Jewish temple would be utterly destroyed.

Archaeological research conducted in Corinth from 1928 to 1947 startled researchers with two objects relating to Paul's epistles to the Corinthian and Roman churches. A Latin inscription dating to about AD 50 carved into an ancient sidewalk identifies Paul's co-laborer Erastus as the city treasurer, which conforms with Paul's account in Romans 16:23. The inscription says that Erastus laid a portion of the sidewalk at his own expense in appreciation for being elected as treasurer. Moreover, a stone platform used to hold public lectures, official business, trials, and to render judgments was unearthed in 1935. It was identified as the *bema* seat. *Bema* is the same Greek word Paul used to describe the judgment seat of Christ (2 Corinthians 5:10), at which all Christians must appear for their rewards (1 Corinthians 3:10–17).[19]

All external evidence—the writings of early Christians, the writings of early non-Christians, and the findings of archaeology—resoundingly confirm that the New Testament is historically reliable. In fact, the examples given in this chapter are just a few selections from a mountain of available evidence showing us that the New Testament is the most thoroughly documented and reinforced writing in all antiquity. And yet there is more to come. The internal evidence test of the Bible adds even more to its already confirmed reliability. That is the subject of the next chapter.

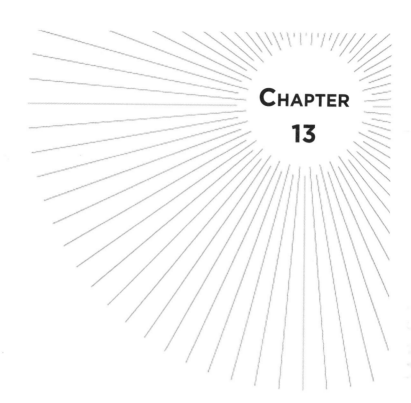

Chapter 13

What about the Errors and Contradictions in Scripture? The Internal Evidence Test

Has anyone ever lied to you? If you've had that experience, your trust in that person was seriously undermined. If someone lies once, how do you know that the person hasn't lied in the past or will lie again in the future? Once deception enters into a relationship, the credibility and integrity of the other person are lost.

It is no different with the writers of the Bible. If exaggerations of the truth, outright lies, errors, or inaccuracies—whether deliberate or accidental—become part of the biblical narrative, then the integrity, credibility, and reliability of the Scripture are lost. One way to check the trustworthiness of the Bible is to determine (1) the extent of internal contradictions and copying errors; (2) whether people have written about things they had little or no firsthand knowledge of; and (3) whether any of the writers claim to have written something that was actually penned by someone else. By addressing these three issues, we will put the Bible to a thorough internal evidence test.

Did Moses Write the Pentateuch?

No other writer of Scripture has been more under question by the critics than Moses. Jewish and conservative Christian scholars have long recognized that Moses wrote the first five books of the Old Testament (the Pentateuch). The dates of his writings are believed to be during the Bronze Age (1500s BC–1200s BC).

Yet, since the mid-1800s of our modern era, critical scholars have contended that the Pentateuch is a collection of writings from numerous sources, by different groups of people, who gathered the information between 850 BC and 445 BC. This view is referred to as the *documentary hypothesis*. The proponents of the documentary hypothesis claim that the period described in the Mosaic narrative (1400 BC) was prior to all knowledge of writing. According to this notion, the books previously ascribed to Moses were actually collected over time and not compiled until sometime around 400 BC. This would, of course, preclude Moses from being the writer because it is almost a thousand years after his death in approximately 1350 BC.

The documentary hypothesis fails to be credible for many reasons, which are extensively explained in *The New Evidence That Demands a Verdict*.[1] In this chapter, we will cite just a few of the internal evidences that demonstrate why the documentary hypothesis is questionable.

In chapter 11 we mentioned the 1976 discovery of the Ebla Tablets by Italian archaeologist Paolo Matthiae. These clay tablets—which numbered more than sixteen thousand—dated from 2400 BC. They delivered a crushing blow to the supposition that writing was nonexistent in the days of Moses and thus he could not have written the Pentateuch. The Ebla findings demonstrate that one thousand years before Moses, there were laws, customs, and events recorded in writing from the same area of the world in which Moses and the patriarchs lived.[2]

Historical critics contended not only that the time of Moses was prior to the invention of writing, but also that the priestly code and legislation recorded in the Pentateuch are too far advanced to have been written by Moses. They alleged that the Israelites at that time were too primitive to have developed anything of such high sophistication, and that it wasn't until about the first half of the Persian period (538 BC–331 BC) that such detailed legislation was recorded.

However, the Ebla tablets containing the law codes demonstrate that elaborate judicial proceedings and case law were in existence centuries before Moses. Many are very similar to the Deuteronomic law code (e.g., Deuteronomy 22:22–30) to which critics have persistently attributed a very late date.[3]

More recent archaeological finds also give credibility to Moses' writings. These discoveries contradict the assumption that the Pentateuch was written hundreds of years after Moses. For example, in 1986, archaeologists in Jerusalem discovered a biblical text older than the Dead Sea Scrolls. Part of the text of Numbers 6:24–26 was written on two small, silver amulets. Gabriel Barkay of Tel Aviv University placed the date of these during the First Temple period, between 960 BC and 586 BC. This again demonstrates that the Pentateuch was complete long before the supposed 400 BC threshold.

Critics have also argued that *Yahweh*—the name for God—was not used before 500 BC–400 BC. If true, this would preclude Moses as the author of the Pentateuch. But the silver amulets contained the name *Yahweh* and were dated before 586 BC, which undercuts the assumption that the Pentateuch was not written by Moses or even in Moses' time.[4]

Critics have further claimed that the Hebrew moral code was too advanced to have been developed by 1200 BC. They say such an advanced social structure could not have come about before the 800s BC. Yet archaeology has uncovered the Akkadian Empire's Code of Hammurabi, dating to before 1200 BC. These laws parallel the laws of Moses, establishing that such advanced moral codes did indeed exist, not only during the time of Moses but prior to it as well.[5]

The documentary hypothesis also assumes that certain difficult expressions and passages from Leviticus would not have been used as early as 1200 BC; therefore the Pentateuch had to have been written much later. As examples, they refer to such terms as "whole burnt offering" (*kalil*), "peace offering" (*shelamin*), and "guilt offering" (*asham*). Yet archaeologists demolished this criticism when they uncovered the Ras Shamra tablets (dated to 1400 BC), which contain a large amount of Ugaritic literature and which include many of the technical sacrificial terms found in Leviticus. This discovery showed that these terms were already current in Palestine at the time of Moses and the conquest. Thus, the entire line of reasoning that claimed a late origin for the terminology of the Levitical cultures is devoid of foundation.[6]

These findings and many others provide overwhelming evidence to support the view that Moses indeed wrote the entire Pentateuch.

Did the Writers of Scripture Have Firsthand Knowledge?

Have you ever read one of those do-it-yourself books? There are a ton of them, on every subject imaginable, from do-it-yourself cabinetmaking, to redecorating your home, to building a doghouse, to repairing your car, to traveling the world on $50 a day. I've often wondered how much some of these do-it-yourself authors really know about their subject. Have they ever built a doghouse, repaired a car, or traveled the world on $50 a day? You would be surprised how many authors write about places they've never been or people they've never met. Some simply do not have firsthand knowledge, or even use primary sources, for their work. They resort to hearsay, legend, or imagination. The use of primary sources is one of the key standards of the internal evidence test for a written document.

Many of the Old Testament writers, such as Isaiah, Ezekiel, Nehemiah, Ezra, and Jeremiah, had firsthand knowledge of what was happening to Israel and what God wanted the people to know. They recorded events that they were participants in and told of their own experiences within those events. The internal evidence test dictates that greater credibility must be granted to writers such as these, who were both geographically and chronologically close to the events they reported. This was certainly the case with the writers of both the Old and New Testaments.

The accounts of Jesus' life, the history of the early church, and the letters that form the bulk of the New Testament were all written by men who were either eyewitnesses to the events they recorded or contemporaries of eyewitnesses. These primary sources lend solid reliability to the New Testament text.

Gospel writers Matthew, Mark, and John could say such things as, "This report is from an eyewitness giving an accurate account" (John 19:35). Luke the physician, who wrote the third Gospel and the book of Acts, affirmed the authenticity of those who wrote about what they heard and saw. "Many people have set out to write accounts about events that have been fulfilled among us. They used the eyewitness reports circulating among us from the early disciples" (Luke 1:1–2). Luke reported these accurate testimonies "so you can be certain of the truth of everything you were taught" (Luke 1:4). Matthew and John were themselves eyewitnesses to the things they wrote, enabling John to say, "We proclaim to you what we ourselves have actually seen and heard" (1 John 1:3). The apostle Peter also was an eyewitness, as he affirms in his second letter: "For we did not follow cunningly devised fables when we made known to you the power and coming of our Lord Jesus Christ, but were eyewitnesses of His majesty" (2 Peter 1:16 NKJV). The apostle Paul, the most prolific New Testament writer, became an eyewitness to Jesus on the road to Damascus and met regularly with other apostles and witnesses to Jesus' life on earth.

Some critics have suggested it would be easy for these early disciples to fabricate stories about Jesus. But F. F. Bruce, the late Rylands Professor of Biblical Criticism at the University of Manchester, disputed this allegation. Concerning the value of the eyewitness accounts of the New Testament records, he writes:

> *The earliest preachers of the gospel knew the value of. . .firsthand testimony, and appealed to it time and again. "We are witnesses of these things," was their constant and confident assertion. And it can have been by no means so easy as some writers seem to think to invent words and deeds of Jesus in those early years, when so many of His disciples were about, who could remember what had and had not happened.*[7]

These eyewitnesses are all the more credible because they appealed to the knowledge of their readers—even their most hostile opponents—who easily could have contradicted any false accounts. Yet these writers of Scripture invited correction by eyewitnesses to their claims when they said such things as the following:

> *"People of Israel, listen! God publicly endorsed Jesus the Nazarene by doing powerful miracles, wonders, and signs through him, as* you well know." *(Acts 2:22, emphasis added)*

> *At this point Festus interrupted Paul's defense. "You are out of your mind, Paul!" he shouted. "Your great learning is driving you insane." "I am not insane, most excellent Festus," Paul replied. "What I am saying is true and reasonable. The king is familiar with these things, and I can speak freely to him. I am convinced that* none of this has escaped his notice, because it was not done in a corner." *(Acts 26:24–26 NIV, emphasis added)*

We find similar appeals in Acts 2:32; 3:15; and 13:31, as well as 1 Corinthians 15:3–8. F. F. Bruce points out, "One of the strong points in the original apostolic preaching is the confident appeal to the knowledge of the hearers; they not only said, 'We are witnesses of these things,' but also, 'As you yourselves also know' (Acts 2:22). Had there been any tendency to depart from the facts in any material respect, the possible presence of hostile witnesses in the audience would have served as a further corrective."[8]

The disciples, in effect, were saying, "Check it out, ask around; you know this as well as we do!" Such challenges demonstrate a supreme confidence that what they recorded was absolutely factual. Bruce summarizes:

"It was not only friendly eyewitnesses that the early preachers had to reckon with; there were others less well-disposed who were also conversant with the main facts of the ministry and death of Jesus. The disciples could not afford to risk inaccuracies (not to speak of willful manipulation of the facts), which would at once be exposed by those who would be only too glad to do so."[9]

The disciples spoke directly to those who violently opposed them, saying, in effect, "You, too, know these facts are true. We dare you to disprove us!" That, of course, would be a foolish approach if they were spreading lies.

Some critics object to this line of evidence, asserting that the writers only claimed to be writing as eyewitnesses or when eyewitnesses were still living. A pseudo-author writing a century or more after the fact could simply claim anything, they say. If the accounts recorded in the Gospels were contrivances of authors much later than the disciples, such writers easily could have concocted not only the miracles of Christ and his resurrection, but also the challenges by Jesus' disciples for their hearers to check out the truthfulness of their accounts.

That's why the dating of the original documents is so important. The fact is, the books of the New Testament are confirmed to have been written during the lifetimes of those involved in the accounts themselves, not a century or more after the events they described. In earlier chapters, we established that the New Testament books were completed no later than AD 100. There are scholars today who would contend that all the books were completed even ten to twenty years earlier. William Foxwell Albright, one of the world's foremost biblical archaeologists, said: "We can already say emphatically that there is no longer any solid basis for dating any book of the New Testament after about AD 80, two full generations before the date between 130 and 150 given by the more radical New Testament critics of today."[10] Albright reiterated this point in a media interview published a few years later.[11] Albright also found that the discoveries of the Dead Sea Scrolls at Qumran confirmed his dating of the New Testament within the lifetimes of Jesus' disciples: "The New Testament proves to be in fact what it was formerly believed to be: the teaching of Christ and his immediate followers between c. AD 25 and c. AD 80."[12]

The fact is, scholars today must regard the New Testament as a legitimate primary source document from the first century. Even many liberal scholars are being forced to consider earlier dates for the New Testament. Anglican bishop and theologian Dr. John A. T. Robinson, who was certainly no conservative scholar, reaches some startling conclusions in his groundbreaking book *Redating the New Testament*. His research convinced him that the whole of the New Testament was written before the fall of Jerusalem in AD 70.[13]

Ample evidence exists to show that, for the most part, the men who wrote the Bible had firsthand knowledge of the events they recorded or access to people who had witnessed those events. We have every reason to believe Scripture passes this primary source standard of the internal evidence test.

Is the Bible Full of Contradictions and Errors?

At some point, you may have heard or read that conservative Christian theologians assert that the Bible is without error (*inerrant*). But many people are confused about what that means. To call the Bible *inerrant* means that when all the facts are known, the Scriptures as they were penned by the writers in the original autographs, and as properly interpreted, will be shown to be true and not false in all they affirm. This would naturally be the case if God is actually the author of Scripture. It stands to reason that if God inspired certain men to reveal his words, he would be sure not to contradict himself, so that his Word would be error-free.

With that said, we are still faced with thousands of biblical manuscripts that are copies of copies of copies of the original autographs. And though the scribes took great care in making accurate copies, some errors were made. Yet that doesn't mean the Bible is full of contradictions and errors as the critics assert.

Such allegations of error in the Bible often flow from a failure to observe the basic standards for interpreting ancient literature. There are certain interpretive principles that guide scholars in discerning whether there is a clear error or a contradiction in any literature. Here are six that are the most critical as they apply to the Bible.

Principle 1: The unexplained is not necessarily unexplainable.

Scientists once had no natural explanation for meteors, eclipses, tornadoes, hurricanes, or earthquakes, but they did not conclude that all things within science were unexplainable. Christian scholars likewise approach the Bible with the same presumption that what is currently *unexplained* isn't *unexplainable*. They simply continue to do research. It is a mistake to assume that what has not yet been explained will *never* be explained.

Principle 2: The context of the passage controls the meaning.

You can prove anything from the Bible if you take words out of context. For example, the Bible says, "There is no God" (Psalm 14:1 NIV). Taken literally, that would constitute a major contradiction. But here's the context: "*The fool says in his heart*, 'There is no God'" (emphasis added). Failure to consider passages in context is one of the major errors of Bible critics.

Principle 3: Clear passages illuminate cloudy ones.

Some Bible passages appear to contradict others. John 3:16 speaks of God's loving the world, while the same author in 1 John 2:15

tells us, "Do not love this world nor the things it offers you." But as we read on in 1 John, we find the clear explanation: John speaks of resisting the evil temptations the world offers, whereas in John 3:16 the clear meaning is that God loves the people of the world. To assume these passages as contradictory is to abandon the common sense we use in interpreting everyday language.

Principle 4: The Bible is a book for humans with human characteristics. Critics point to Psalm 19:6 as an obvious case of the Bible's fallibility: "The sun rises at one end of the heavens and follows its course to the other end." We've known for centuries that the sun does not move around the earth; the earth's rotation merely causes the sun to appear to move. The same critic can speak in the next breath of watching a beautiful "sunset," ignoring the fact that a term can be nonscientific without being inaccurate. The Bible uses nontechnical, everyday figures of speech, common expressions, and well-known literary devices. It uses round numbers in some places and exact numbers in others. None of these instances of normal use of language amounts to a contradiction.

Principle 5: An incomplete report is not a false report.
Mark 5:1–20 and Luke 8:26–39 speak of Jesus' encounter with a demoniac in Gadara, whereas the parallel account in Matthew 8:28–34 tells us there were two demoniacs. Is this a contradiction? Mark and Luke, neither of whom were eyewitnesses to the event, could have recorded a report that focused on the more prominent of two demoniacs and ignored the other. Their accounts may be less complete, but they are not contradictory. Matthew simply supplies more information.

Principle 6: Errors in copies do not equate to errors in the originals.
We have already touched on this principle. Simply stated, scholars are able to determine many of the copyists' errors by common sense and by comparing later copies with earlier copies. It stands to reason that those copies that are closer in time to the originals are likely to be the more accurate.

Examining Some Errors and Apparent Contradictions

With the above interpretive principles in mind, let's look at some supposed errors and apparent contradictions in Scripture.

Most biblical scholars simply accept that there are spelling differences and incorrect numbers in Scripture. For example, some manuscripts of the New Testament spell the name John with one *n*; other times it is spelled with two. Technically this constitutes an error, but it certainly is a minor one.

Nehemiah 2:19 refers to a man called Geshem the Arab; but a few chapters later, his name is spelled "Gashmu" (Nehemiah 6:6). This appears to be an error. Yet upon closer examination, we find it is simply a difference in the form of proper names between Hebrew and Arabic. In Nehemiah 2:19, the Hebrew version of the name is used; in Nehemiah 6:6, the Arabic name is given. Though at first this appears to be an error, it actually is not.

At other times, there are actual errors made by the scribes who copied the Hebrew text. They were human, and a tired and sleepy scribe would be prone to copy the wrong numbers. For example, in some Greek manuscripts and Syriac versions, it says that King Ahaziah was forty-two years old when he began to reign in Jerusalem (see 2 Chronicles 22:2). Yet 2 Kings 8:26 says that Ahaziah was twenty-two years old when he began his reign.

The reality is, King Ahaziah could not have been forty-two at the time, for that would make him older than his own father. Joram, his father, became king at the age of thirty-two, before his son was king. Joram died eight years later at the age of forty. Ahaziah was obviously twenty-two as reported in 2 Kings, and it's clear that the copyist of 2 Chronicles 22:2 was in error.

In 2 Chronicles 9:25, some manuscripts read that King Solomon had 4,000 horse stalls for the 1,400 chariots he owned, as described in both 1 Kings 10:26 and 2 Chronicles 1:14. Yet in 1 Kings 4:26, some Greek manuscripts state that Solomon had "40,000 stalls of horses." Would the king need 40,000 stalls to accommodate just 1,400 chariots? Not likely. It is more likely that a scribe mistakenly added an extra zero to the figure of 4,000 horse stalls.

A similar manuscript copying error is found in 1 Samuel 13:5, where it says that the Philistines had 30,000 chariots and 6,000 chariot drivers. Naturally one wonders why they would have so many chariots and so few chariot drivers. The Syriac (Aramaic) manuscripts and some versions of the Greek Septuagint put the chariot count at 3,000. That is the most likely number, and the error of the extra zero is no doubt a slip of the pen by a scribe. Of course, all subsequent manuscripts were copied from the altered one and the error was carried forward.

These types of copying errors are understandable and do not substantively change the meaning of the text. However, there are apparent contradictions in Scripture that seem truly problematic. As we have stated, clear contradictions within the original text would be paramount to God contradicting himself. And critics are quick to point to a number of these apparent contradictions. But upon closer examination, these supposed discrepancies can be resolved.

For example, Matthew's report of one angel at Jesus' tomb (Matthew 28:2) seems to vary from Luke's report that two angels were there (Luke 24:4). Critics will say this is a biblical contradiction. Actually, it isn't at all. Matthew doesn't say there was *only* one angel at the tomb. If he did, that would contradict Luke's report. Matthew merely identifies one angel, most likely the one who spoke.

This is no more a contradiction than if you told me you went to the grocery store yesterday, and then in a later conversation you told me your friend went with you. I couldn't accuse you of contradicting yourself in such a case. Because one of the principles of interpretation is that an incomplete report is not a false report. So the lack of additional information as to who went with you to the store doesn't make your first statement false. Neither are Luke's and Matthew's reports about one or two angels contradictory.

Other apparent contradictions are more challenging. An example is the differing accounts by Matthew and Peter explaining the death of Judas. In Acts 1, we read Peter's account: "Judas had bought a field with the money he received for his treachery. Falling headfirst there, his body split open, spilling out all his intestines" (Acts 1:18). Matthew's account seems quite different. He reports the death this way: "Judas threw the silver coins down in the Temple and went out and hanged himself" (Matthew 27:5). The two accounts are contradictory, right? Actually, they're not.

Matthew does not say that Judas did not fall; neither does Peter say that Judas did not hang himself. This is not a matter of one person being right and the other person wrong. Both accounts can be true, with one merely supplementing what is told in the other.

A plausible explanation would be this: Judas hanged himself on a tree on the edge of a precipice that overlooked the field he bought. After he hung there for some time—or perhaps due to the sudden weight of his body at the moment of hanging—the limb of the tree snapped or the rope gave way and he fell down the ledge, mangling his body in the process.

The fall could have come before or after Judas's death, as either would fit this explanation. This possibility is entirely natural when the terrain of the valley in that area is examined. From the bottom of the valley, the rocky terraces are between twenty-five and forty feet high and the cliffs below them are almost perpendicular.

To this day there are still trees that grow around the ledges, with a rocky surface at the bottom. Therefore, it is easy to conclude that Judas struck one of the jagged rocks on his way down, tearing his body open. Matthew and Peter provide different perspectives of Judas's death, but they are not contradictory.

Here's a question: Who in the Old Testament killed Goliath the giant? Practically everyone knows that one—David killed Goliath, as it is recorded in 1 Samuel 17:50–51. Yet in 2 Samuel, the Masoretic text from which many of our English Bibles are translated says that Elhanan "killed Goliath the Gittite" (2 Samuel 21:19 NASB). This appears to be a clear contradiction of the scriptural record.

Yet 1 Chronicles gives record of the same battle as 2 Samuel, and it states that Elhanan "killed Lahmi the brother of Goliath the Gittite" (1 Chronicles 20:5 NASB). This indicates that a copyist of 2 Samuel 21:19 erred by leaving out the words "Lahmi the brother of" in the Masoretic text. If you have a more recent translation, such as the New International Version or the New Living Translation, you will probably note that the translators have corrected the error by adding the words "Lahmi the brother of" to the text.

Dr. Gleason L. Archer was a respected biblical scholar, theologian, and educator who served on the teams that translated the New American Standard Bible (NASB) and the New International Version (NIV). He was a gifted seminary professor, fluent in twenty-seven languages. Dr. Archer gave this testimony about the internal evidence of the Bible in the forward to his *Encyclopedia of Bible Difficulties*:

As I have dealt with one apparent discrepancy after another and have studied the alleged contradictions between the biblical record and the evidence of linguistics, archaeology, or science, my confidence in the trustworthiness of Scripture has been repeatedly verified and strengthened by the discovery that almost every problem in Scripture that has ever been discovered by man, from ancient times until now, has been dealt with in a completely satisfactory manner by the biblical text itself—or else by objective archaeological information. . . . There is a good and sufficient answer in Scripture itself to refute every charge that has been leveled against it.[14]

We can be confident that the biblical text is free of known contradictions, and in fact is rooted in the accounts of eyewitnesses. The Bible passes the internal evidence test. When you hold a Bible in your hands and read its words, you can be assured you are receiving the message from God's heart to yours.

But is it possible that God could speak through the writings of other religions? Is God so exclusive that he couldn't have inspired other writers of different faiths to communicate his message as well? Let's grapple with that issue in the next chapter.

Are Writings from Other Religions Considered Scripture?

God created a very diverse world. Just look at the variety in plant and animal life. Have you ever seen two people who are exactly the same in looks, build, personality, or thought processes? Even identical twins have more differences than you can imagine. We all exhibit distinct personalities and have different perspectives on life. So wouldn't it stand to reason that a God of diversity would share his truth through numerous religious sources? He wouldn't choose just one Bible and one religion through which to reveal himself and his truth, would he? That would be quite exclusive of him, and in our world today, exclusivity is a huge no-no.

Pew Research published a demographic study in December 2012 titled "The Global Religious Landscape." The report shows that a little less than one-third (32 percent) of the world's population is Christian; 23 percent are Muslim, 15 percent Hindu, 7 percent Buddhist, 0.2 percent Jewish, and just under 7 percent practice various folk or traditional religions, including African traditional religions, Chinese folk religions, Native American religions, and religions such as the Bahá'i faith, Jainism, Sikhism, Taoism, Wicca, etc. Roughly 16 percent have no religious affiliation at all.[1]

Over half the world's population turns to some source other than the Judeo-Christian Scriptures for teaching and inspiration from their god or higher power. So it's only natural that you might ask: "Josh, are you going to claim there is only one way to God, and he has limited himself to one written revelation of himself—the Bible?"

Obviously, if I made that assertion, I would be saying that Christianity and the Bible are utterly exclusive. I would be declaring that more than 50 percent of the world's population has it wrong. It may surprise some people that *I* just can't make that claim. Who am *I* to say that *my* religion as revealed in the Bible is the only one and true religion? Now, before you judge me on this, allow me to add quickly that I do believe that the God-breathed words of Scripture are the only revelation of the one true God. But I am not the one who actually makes that claim—God himself does. He is the one who claims to be the one true God and that Scripture is his true revelation to humanity. I have simply chosen to believe him and his Word.

God Said He Is the One and Only

When Moses came down from speaking with God on Mount Sinai more than three thousand years ago, he said to the children of Israel:

> *"[God] showed you these things so you would know that the LORD is God and there is no other. He let you hear his voice from heaven so he could instruct you. He let you see his great fire here on earth so he could speak to you from it. . . . So remember this and keep it firmly in mind: The LORD is God both in heaven and on earth, and there is no other." (Deuteronomy 4:35–36, 39)*

Moses spoke with this God who had no equal. He told Moses he was "the God of Abraham, the God of Isaac, and the God of Jacob" (Exodus 3:15). He would later reveal himself to the prophet Isaiah and say, "I alone am God! I am God, and there is none like me. Only I can tell you the future before it even happens. Everything I plan will come to pass, for I do whatever I wish" (Isaiah 46:9–10). It is this God who "is the everlasting God, the Creator of all the earth" (Isaiah 40:28).

This same God revealed himself to Moses and the prophets and inspired them to write the five books of the law (Pentateuch), the eight prophetic books, and the eleven writings. Then, hundreds of years after he revealed himself to Moses and the prophets, he revealed himself in another, much more personal and spectacular way: "The Word became human and made his home among us. He was full of unfailing love and faithfulness. And we have seen his glory, the glory of the Father's one and only Son" (John 1:14). It was this human, Jesus, whom John calls the Word, who told us that he was the one the ancient prophecies had predicted. There were sixty major Old Testament prophecies, with about 270 additional ramifications, fulfilled in this one man called Jesus, the Christ. This was the God of Abraham, Isaac, and Jacob who took on human skin. After he was crucified, died, and rose again, he told his disciples:

> *"When I was with you before, I told you that everything written about me in the law of Moses and the prophets and in the Psalms must be fulfilled." Then he opened their minds to understand the Scriptures. And he said, "Yes, it was written long ago that the Messiah would suffer and die and rise from the dead on the third day. It was also written that this message would be proclaimed in the authority of his name to all the nations, beginning in Jerusalem: 'There is forgiveness of sins for all who repent.' You are witnesses of all these things." (Luke 24:44–48)*

Jesus was referring to the prophecies of Isaiah, Joel, and Amos, which told of the redemptive plan of the one true God to send his Son as a sacrifice for all who believe in him. The Law, the Prophets, and the Psalms (the Writings) all point to this same God taking on human form to die and rise again, so that humans can be reconnected to God—raised to new life forever in relationship with Christ.

As we can see, Christianity isn't an exclusive religion concocted by a group of fanatics called Christians. It is a revelation *to all humanity* by the God of Abraham, Isaac, and Jacob. It was not fallible humans who claimed its exclusivity; it was the Creator God in the flesh himself:

*"I am the resurrection and the life. Those who believe in
me even though they die like everyone else, will live again.
They are given eternal life for believing in me and will
never perish." (John 11:25–26)*

*"Unless you believe that I Am who I claim to be, you will
die in your sins." (John 8:24)*

*"I am the way, the truth, and the life. No one can come to
the Father except through me." (John 14:6)*

For good reason, Jesus made the exclusive claim that he is the only
way to God. No other human had the qualifications to be the holy and
perfect sacrifice for the sins of the world, except the God-man Jesus.
The Old and New Testament Scriptures record God's exclusive plan
to redeem humans—which, in effect, excludes all other religions and
their writings as a means of salvation.

No Other God, No Other Bible

People have asked me, "What about Allah as God, and the Qur'an as
the Bible? Isn't Allah the same as the Christians' God and the Qur'an
a book of good teachings? Isn't this simply a different path that God
has made to enable people to reach him?"

It's true that Muslims believe the Qur'an is a revelation from God
(*Allah*). They believe that revelation was verbally transmitted through
the angel Gabriel to Muhammad, beginning when he was forty years
old (AD 610). They say that Muhammad received these messages,
which he precisely memorized, over a twenty-three-year period.
Shortly after Muhammad's death (AD 632), the Qur'an was compiled
into a single book. Today it is divided into 114 chapters, or *suras*, and is
about the length of the Christian New Testament. Muslims consider

the Qur'an in the original Arabic text to be the literal word of God. They believe it provides divine guidance for all humanity. They say Muhammad was God's last prophet, superseding Christ, and that the Qur'an is God's final revelation to us all.

But does the Qur'an portray Allah as a Supreme Being who is the same as the God of the Christian Bible?

The Bible says that Moses specifically asked God to identify himself. Moses was concerned that his people in Egypt would want to know God's name to be sure who authorized Moses to lead them. "And God said to Moses, 'I AM WHO I AM' [Yahweh]; and He said, 'Thus you shall say to the sons of Israel, "I AM [Yahweh] has sent me to you"'" (Exodus 3:14 NASB). The Qur'an never refers to Allah as Yahweh, yet the Old Testament uses Yahweh as God's name more than 6,800 times.

There is another significant distinction between Allah of the Qur'an and Yahweh of the Christian Bible. It is recorded in the book of Luke that an angel came to Mary and told her that as a virgin she would give birth to a child. The angel said, "So the baby to be born will be holy, and he will be called the Son of God" (Luke 1:35). Even though a sincere Muslim would adamantly disagree with this distinction, the Bible claims that Yahweh has an eternal Son who took on human form in the person of Jesus.

Beyond these two distinctions, there is an important difference in the character of the Supreme Being presented in the Qur'an as compared with the God of the Christian Bible. It is true that the Qur'an portrays Allah as eternal, all-powerful, all-knowing, holy, just, and merciful just as the Bible does regarding Yahweh. But the Qur'an claims that these are characteristics of Allah's *will* rather than his nature. In other words, Allah may be called good because he causes good, but goodness is not the essence of his character.

The Bible, however, reveals an altogether different God. Scripture reveals the nature and essence of God, Yahweh, as one who "is good and does what is right" (Psalm 25:8). He is "the one who is holy and true" (Revelation 3:7). "He is the Rock; his deeds are perfect. Everything he does is just and fair. He is a faithful God who does no wrong; how just and upright he is!" (Deuteronomy 32:4). "The LORD is righteous in everything he does; he is filled with kindness" (Psalm 145:17). "The LORD is just! He is my rock! There is no evil in him!" (Psalm 92:15). Goodness and righteousness are the very essence of who God is—not characteristics he adopts based on a momentary whim. These characteristics are the core of his nature. It is clear that the Bible and the Qur'an represent two very different views of God, as the following story portrays.

Some time ago, I was in South Africa, sharing evidence for the Christian faith with Muslims. In one of my talks, I made a point about the consistency of God's character of goodness. I said that he always acts according to his righteous nature. What he *does* is always consistent with who he *is*.

After my talk, a young Muslim approached me. "Your concept of God," he said, "is not my concept of Allah. Allah is all-powerful. Allah's powers can allow him to do anything."

"Can Allah lie and cheat?" I asked.

"Sure," he responded. "Allah can do all things. He is not limited like your God. If he wants to love, he loves. If he wants to hate, he hates. Allah is all-powerful."

"Could Allah punish you for something you did," I asked, "even if it were good?"

"If Allah did not like it, he would punish me."

"Then you don't always know how Allah might respond, do you?"

He thought for a moment. "No," he said. "I don't always know what he would do." He stopped but added quickly, "But I do know Allah is all-powerful."

I nodded. "You see, if I served Allah, I would be serving him out of fear. If he exercised the power to do wrong as well as right, simply because he desired to at the moment, he would be punishing me from his own selfish desires. That would be a dreadful motivation from which to serve him, because I would never know what angered him." The young man was listening intently, so I continued. "You see, I serve God out of love. The fact that he is holy and perfect and almighty is worthy of my fear—my respect. But because I know he is merciful and always acts consistent with his loving nature, I serve him out of love. I always know what angers him, and I always know what pleases him, because he always remains consistent by his very nature."

I walked away from that conversation even more in awe of the God I serve. He can always be counted on to act lovingly, because it's in his unchanging nature to do so. The God revealed in Scripture is the one we can count on to be there for us and always do right by us. "He remains faithful," Scripture says, "for he cannot deny who he is" (2 Timothy 2:13).

Being holy and right aren't things that God *decides* to do; they are something he *is*. All that is right and holy and just and good is derived from his core nature—his essence. Scripture says, "Whatever is good and perfect is a gift coming down to us from God our Father, who created all the lights in the heavens" (James 1:17).

If other writings depict God as different from the holy and righteous God who revealed himself to Moses and the prophets, obviously it isn't the same God. "I alone am God! I am God, and there is none like me" (Isaiah 46:9). People, groups, or other religions may continue to depict their gods differently from the God revealed in Scripture. But as Scripture clearly tells us, they are all false gods. I for one have chosen to base my belief in the God revealed in the God-breathed words of Scripture.

Even within the broad category of Christianity, there are differing views on whether the Bible is the only true revelation of God. Some believe there are other books that are inspired by God and equal in authority to the sixty-six books of the Bible. As mentioned earlier, the Roman Catholic Church has accepted the fourteen books of the Apocrypha as equal to the other books of Scripture. The Church of Jesus Christ of Latter-day Saints (LDS) accepts the Book of Mormon as equal to Scripture. But is the Book of Mormon the God-breathed, inspired words of God?

To answer that question, let's review the canon that we introduced previously—the four guidelines that church leaders used to recognize whether a writing is, in fact, God-inspired.

1. The writing was authored by an apostle or prophet of God or by someone closely connected with one or more of the apostles or prophets.
2. The writings clearly evidenced the confirming power and presence of God.
3. The message was consistent with other recognized Scripture.
4. The writing was widely accepted by the church from an early date.

Let's see how the Book of Mormon measures up to the guidelines of the canon.

In 1827, Mormon founder Joseph Smith claimed that an angel named Moroni informed him of a set of gold plates buried in a hill in present-day New York. These plates were said to have ancient writings engraved on them. Smith said he uncovered these plates, and after translating them, he had them published as the Book of Mormon in 1830.

The LDS Church bases many of its beliefs on the Book of

Mormon. But they also claim that several other books are equally inspired. Joseph Smith claimed to have had an encounter with Jesus, in which Jesus revealed many other things to him. These revelations were published in the Doctrine and Covenants. The accounts of Smith's interaction with Jesus and his story of discovering gold plates are found in a third book, Pearl of Great Price. These three documents, along with the Bible and continuing revelations, form the basis of LDS beliefs. Since the death of Joseph Smith in 1844, these documents have been supplemented by other revelations that the LDS Church says have been given to its leaders. However, the LDS officially considers the Book of Mormon as the "most correct" book of scripture.

The Book of Mormon is written in a King James Bible historic style and tells about two ancient civilizations that supposedly migrated to the American continent. The first group was said to be composed of refugees from the Tower of Babel, and the second group came from Jerusalem around 600 BC. The first group was eventually destroyed because of its corruption. The second group, under the leadership of a man named Nephi, was made up of God-fearing Jews, and they prospered. However, some of the people ceased to worship the true God, and they received the curse of dark skin—these people were said to be Native Americans, earlier called Indians.

The Book of Mormon claims that after Jesus' resurrection, he visited America and revealed himself to the followers of Nephi. Eventually, this group was destroyed by the Indians around AD 428. Joseph Smith claimed that these accounts were written on the gold plates he found and translated as the Book of Mormon.

Mormons believe the Bible is true "insofar as it is correctly translated." But they also accept their three church writings as God-inspired. Additionally, Mormons believe their church leaders continue to receive God-inspired revelations. So, in essence, new "revelations from God" supersede previous revelations.

The Book of Mormon, the Doctrine and Covenants, Pearl of Great Price, and the continuing revelations of the LDS Church leaders form Mormon theology and teachings. Both the LDS Church as an institution and its members present themselves as a part of the Christian faith and actually believe they are the only true church. The theology of the Mormons, however, is not that of Christianity taught from the Old and New Testament Scriptures. For example, the LDS Church teaches the following:

- God the Father was once a human and today has flesh and bones rather than being a spirit as Jesus said God is (John 4:24).
- Humans are destined to evolve into godhood. The Mormon saying is, "As man is, God once was: as God is, man may become." The Bible teaches that we are to be transformed into God's likeness rather than evolving into godhood (see Ephesians 4:23–24 and 1 John 3:2).
- Works are the basis of salvation and will determine what kind of position and place we have in heaven. This contradicts the biblical view that we are justified by grace through faith in Jesus (see Romans 3:27–28 and Ephesians 2:8).
- Scripture is not the final revelation of God—rather, the leaders of the LDS Church receive continuing revelations that are equal to and even supersede the Old and New Testament Scriptures.[2]

As you can see, the Book of Mormon fails to measure up to the rules of the canon on a number of counts, if not on all counts. Most notably, it is inconsistent with Scripture. Taking into account the other Mormon documents for which inspiration is claimed, Mormonism is inconsistent with itself in that later writings supersede earlier ones. This means the Mormon god is not the perfect and consistent Christian God, for the Mormon god changes and corrects himself. The true God, on the other hand, "never changes or casts a shifting shadow" (James 1:17). Furthermore, the historical events claimed by Mormonism (the migrations to America, visits by Jesus and angels, and the finding of the golden plates) have no corroborating external evidence to validate them. They are simply the unsubstantiated claims of one man.

God's Word, the inspired Scripture, is true because God is true. It reveals the Creator God, the one true and mighty God who has no equal. Believing that does not make a person narrow-minded or exclusive. It merely means that God has declared himself the only true God, and that the only way to him is through his Son, Jesus Christ, and the person has elected to believe him.

The apostle John said, "Dear friends, do not believe everyone who claims to speak by the Spirit. You must test them to see if the spirit they have comes from God. For there are many false prophets in the world" (1 John 4:1). We are to test the spirits of other religions and questionable doctrines and groups against the truth of Scripture. The Bible is God's revelation of himself. When any view or idea does not measure up to the God of the Bible and the truth of Scripture, we can know it is false.

We have covered a lot of ground over these past fourteen chapters. In the next and last chapter, I would like to share with you a way to approach Scripture that may be fresh and new to you. When someone shared it with me, it made all the difference in the world to me in allowing God to work in my life. God's Word is "alive and powerful," and he wants his truth to come alive in your life.

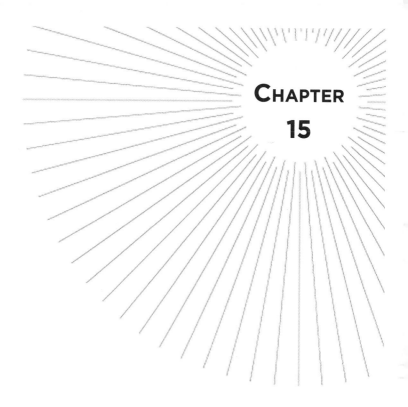

CHAPTER

15

How the Bible Can Come Alive in Your Life

"You come out here right now," the man commanded with a stern voice. When the child appeared, the father said, "I told you to clean up this garage, and it hasn't been touched. Why haven't you obeyed me?"

Have you ever heard the voice of an inspecting dad or the disappointed tone of a distraught mother? Most of us grew up receiving correction for those things we didn't do properly. How that correction was handed out and how we received it can dramatically affect our sense of acceptance. And for many who experienced authoritative parents, that sense of acceptance naturally became performance-based.

One of the biggest mistakes people make is reading the Bible through a distorted lens of past experiences. That approach skews our view of God and our relationship with him.

Research in the field of how we form relationships has led psychologists to what is known as *attachment theory*. The concept is that we were born with the need to make secure attachments with others. We will inevitably make attachments, and if we can't make secure attachments, we make insecure ones—even if they negatively affect our lives.

Mark Matlock, president of WisdomWorks Ministries, asks: "If insecure human attachments keep us from healthy connections with others, couldn't they keep us from connecting with God as well?"[1]

Our perception of God is generally colored by our child-to-parent relationships, especially the child-to-father relationship. How you related to your parents has no doubt greatly influenced your perception of God. For example, if you grew up with authoritarian parents and felt their disapproval, you may tend to project those feelings into your relationship with God. It is natural to bring that distorted lens to your reading of Scripture, causing you to see God as an authoritarian and disapproving figure.

I have come across a lot of Christians who study the Bible with an "inspecting and/or disappointed God" lens. They seem to ask at least three questions about practically every passage they read:

1. *What sin here needs to be avoided? (As if an inspecting God is watching them critically.)*
2. *What commandments here need to be obeyed? (As if a demanding God requires immediate obedience.)*
3. *What part of my life has to change? (As if a disappointed God requires perfect performance.)*

It is not that we shouldn't avoid sin or understand what biblical commands we need to obey. But when we view God's Word through the lens of a disappointed and inspecting God, we distort his truth. Paul told the Christ-followers in Ephesus that he was praying that God would "give you the Spirit of wisdom and revelation, so that you may know [Jesus] better. . .that the eyes of your heart may be enlightened in order that you may know the hope to which he has called you" (Ephesians 1:17–18 NIV).

In this passage, the Greek word for "wisdom" is *ophia*, which refers to wisdom in spiritual truth providing insight into the true nature of things. The word *revelation* is from the Greek *apokalupsis*, which means the uncovering or unveiling of the knowledge of God to the soul. In other words, when Paul prays that the eyes of our hearts would be enlightened, he is asking God to peel back the distorted view we have of God and to let us see the true nature of who Jesus is until it penetrates deep into our souls.

God wants to open the eyes of our hearts to see him for who he is. He wants to purge our minds and emotions of the false image of a disappointed or inspecting God that may have been placed there by past or present unhealthy relationships. He wants his God-breathed words to cleanse and rectify any distortions we may have of him. When this is done, we can experience God as he meant us to experience him.

Again, I must give credit to my friend David Ferguson for the insights in the next section. David's work on Relational Christology has significantly impacted by view of Christ and his Word. See David's *Relational Foundations* resource at www.relationshippress.com

What Kind of God Do You See?

Journey with me back to the time when Jesus celebrated his last Passover meal with his disciples. The story is recorded in John 14. He tells the twelve men assembled there, "If you love Me, you will keep My commandments" (John 14:15 NASB).

Now, suppose for a moment that you are in the group with the Twelve, and as Jesus speaks these words he makes eye contact with you. In your mind and in your emotions, how would you respond to his statement? Why would Jesus be saying these words to you? How you hear the words of Jesus in this biblical narrative is very telling.

Is Jesus Disappointed?

What do *you* hear in Jesus' voice as he makes his statement about love and commandments? Do you possibly hear it through some past feeling of false guilt? Do you see Jesus crossing his arms and shaking his head, saying, "If you really loved me, you would have kept my commandments all along. Your failings before, and even now, speak volumes. I know you are trying to please me, but you are such a disappointment."

If you sense his disappointment, you might compensate by working harder at performing for God in hopes of feeling worthy of his love. The problem is, *no one* can live the Christian life perfectly. If we sense in Scripture a disappointed God, we will tend to see his love as a reward for our good performance. This may cause us to see only the "thou shalt nots" of the Bible and miss its many promises. This view sets up our emotions to feel, *I must do right to be loved right.* Invariably, this perception will affect all our relationships.

Is Jesus Inspecting You?

When Jesus says, "If you love me, you will keep my commandments," do you see him raising his eyebrows and hear him emphasizing the first word?

"*If* you love me. . ."

Do you hear a questioning tone in his voice, as if his statement were really something of a warning: "Do you know that I'm watching you to see if you keep my commandments?"

Some see God in just this way—as an inspector who grades us on how well we follow the directives in the Bible. Is that the kind of God you see? Is he one who stands over you with a pad and pencil, keeping a running tally of all your deeds, both good and bad? It's hard to imagine this kind of God celebrating who you are or being happy just to be with you. His scrutinizing, inspecting eye would sap the joy out of the relationship.

If we see God as an inspector, we might tend to take even the slightest corrective suggestion from others as a personal attack and become defensive. We also may be prone to take on the role of inspector ourselves and suspiciously monitor the behavior of others. We might make big deals out of minor biblical issues. As you can imagine, people find it difficult to enjoy the fellowship of someone who keeps them under scrutiny and records any deviation from the letter of the law.

Is Jesus Accepting of You?

When you hear Jesus' statement, do you perceive an accepting God? Your eyes meet. This is your Savior, who sees you just the way you are and loves and accepts you beyond your wildest dreams. He tells you there are many rooms in his Father's house, and he is going to prepare a place for you. Then he makes you a promise: "I will come and get you, so that you will always be with me where I am" (John 14:3).

Jesus now explains that the works he has done were actually not of his own doing: it was the Father working through him. And he makes you another promise: "Anyone who believes in me will do the same works I have done" (John 14:12).

He smiles reassuringly and gives you yet another promise: "You can ask for anything in my name, and I will do it" (John 14:13). Do any of these promises sound like something coming from a disappointed or inspecting Jesus? They are coming from the One who welcomes you and receives you with a full embrace and without reservation or conditions. Then, in a tender voice with accepting eyes, he makes you a final promise. Listen to his words as he extends his arms toward you and with a smile on his face says, "If you love Me, you will keep My commandments" (John 14:15 NASB).

This is the beginning statement of a very special promise to you. It is meant to bring you reassurance, security, and confidence. Listen to the actual promise in the next two verses: "I will ask the Father, and he will give you another Advocate, who will never leave you. He is the Holy Spirit, who leads into all truth" (John 14:16–17). Doesn't this give you incredible confidence? In effect, Jesus is saying, "If you and I have a loving relationship, I promise I am not going to leave you alone to try to live the Christian life in your own strength. I'm going to take up residence in your life through the power and person of my Holy Spirit, and I will be there to empower you. I will be there to give you the joy in life that I have always intended for you." Remember, he adds, "I have told you this so that my joy may be in you and that your joy may be complete" (John 15:11 NIV).

This is the promise that comes to us from the accepting Jesus. And when we embrace his biblical promise, his love becomes real to us. In fact, it is his transforming love that enables us to love him back so deeply and to love each other as Jesus loves us.

Lay aside any preconceived ideas of God based on your past relationships with others, and allow Scripture to define the accepting

Jesus. He loves every one of us in spite of our sin—including *you*. He has mercifully provided atonement for our sin at great cost to himself. He separates who we are from what we have done and loves us for who we are. Then he accepts—receives with welcoming arms—each of us at the point of our failure.

That is the God the Bible reveals. Receive his unconditional acceptance and experience freedom from false guilt and self-condemnation. Respond to the welcoming embrace of the Savior and rest in his secure arms. Reach out and grasp his promise and be infused with his Holy Spirit, who empowers you to live a life pleasing to him.[2]

If the God-breathed words of Scripture are to come alive in our lives, we must see Jesus for who he is—the God who loves and accepts us without condition based on what Christ did on the cross. He is there with outstretched arms, longing to lead us through his Word so we can know him more intimately. Seeing God through a lens other than the loving and accepting Jesus will distort his truth, and his truth will become irrelevant to our lives.

Jesus made a unique offer to those who heard him in person two thousand years ago. He makes you and me the same offer today. Listen to what he says:

> *"Come to me, all you who are weary and burdened, and I will give you rest. Take my yoke upon you and learn from me, for I am gentle and humble in heart, and you will find rest for your souls." (Matthew 11:28–29 NIV)*

Jesus wants you yoked (linked together) with him so closely that you can *learn* of him. He wants you to learn who he truly is and how much he loves you. He wants you to find true rest for your soul. As you read his Word, seek to know how each passage provides a fresh understanding of who God is. Discover God's heart and motives within the pages of Scripture. Explore how the Bible tells you of a God who loves you dearly and one you can love without reservation. See how Jesus accepts you and wants to love others through you. View God's Word as a means to know God, and he will empower you to live as you ought to live. "As [you] know Jesus better," the apostle Peter writes, "his divine power gives [you] everything [you] need for living a godly life" (2 Peter 1:3).

God's Word is "alive and powerful." It is the expression of God's heart to yours. It is reliable and trustworthy. It is the word of truth and life. Know his Word. Experience his Word. Share his Word with others. "Heaven and earth will disappear," Jesus said, "but my words remain forever" (Matthew 24:35 TLB).

Notes

CHAPTER 1

1. Experian Marketing Services 2013 Digital Marketer Report, www.experian.com/marketing-services/2013-digital-marketer-report.html.

2. Ingrid Lunden, "Facebook Passes 1B Mobile Users, 200M Messenger Users in Q1," TechCrunch, April 23, 2014, http://techcrunch.com/2014/04/23/facebook-passes-1b-mobile-monthly-active-users-in-q1-as-mobile-ads-reach-59-of-all-ad-sales/.

3. "Connecting with Kids Online," eMarketer Digital Intelligence, February 9, 2011, www.emarketer.com/Article/Connecting-with-Kids-Online/1008227.

CHAPTER 3

1. Drawn from David Ferguson, *Relational Foundations: Experience Relevance in Life and Ministry* (Austin, TX: Relational Press, 2004), 69-104.

2. Insights from David Ferguson, *The Great Commandment Principle* (Austin, TX: Relational Press, 1998), 10-18.

CHAPTER 5

1. S. I. McMillen, MD, *None of These Diseases* (Westwood, NJ: Spire, 1968), preface.

2. Adapted from Josh and Dottie McDowell, *Straight Talk with Your Kids about Sex* (Eugene, OR: Harvest House, 2012), 38.

3. David Ferguson, *Top Ten Relational Needs* and *Intimate Encounters*, found at www.relationshippress.com

CHAPTER 7

1. Alan Hirsch, *The Forgotten Ways: Reactivating the Missional Church* (Grand Rapids: Brazos, 2006), 18.

2. Josh McDowell, *The New Evidence That Demands a Verdict* (Nashville: Thomas Nelson, 1999), 21–22.

3. Ibid., 26.

CHAPTER 8

1. *Merriam-Webster's Collegiate Dictionary*, 10th ed., s.v. "unique."

2. Joab Jackson, "Google: 129 Million Different Books Have Been Published," IDG News Service, August 6, 2010, www.pcworld.com /article/202803/google_129_million_different_books_have_been _published.html.

3. United Bible Societies, "'Great Strides' in Bible Translation and Scripture Access in 2013," July 24, 2014. Search "great strides" at www .biblesociety.org.

4. United Bible Societies, "Scripture Distribution Increases in Persecution Hotspots," November 22, 2013. Search "scripture distribution increases" at www.biblesociety.org.

5. Josh McDowell, *The New Evidence That Demands a Verdict* (Nashville: Thomas Nelson, 1999), 9.

6. Ibid., 10.

7. Ibid.

8. Ibid., 11.

9. Ibid.

CHAPTER 9

1. Josh McDowell, *The New Evidence That Demands a Verdict* (Nashville: Thomas Nelson, 1999), 18.

2. Ibid.

CHAPTER 10

1. Virginia Brown, *The Textual Transmission of Caesar's Civil War* (Leiden, Netherlands: Brill, 1972), introduction.

2. Ibid.

3. Ibid.

4. F. F. Bruce, *The New Testament Documents: Are They Reliable?* (Downers Grove, IL: InterVarsity, 1964), 16; and personal correspondence between Clay Jones and Daniel Wallace, January 13, 2012.

5. Leuven Database of Ancient Books; www.trismegistos.org/ldab /search.php. See also R. A. McNeal, *Herodotus: Book I* (New York: University Press, 1986), 13.

6. Bruce, *New Testament Documents*, 16.

7. Robert M. Horn, *The Book That Speaks for Itself* (Downers Grove, IL: InterVarsity, 1970), 86–87.

8. Dan Brown, *The DaVinci Code* (New York: Doubleday, 2003), 231.

CHAPTER 11

1. Martin L. West, *Studies in the Text and Transmission of the Iliad* (Munich: K. G. Saur, 2011), 86. Clay Jones, personal correspondence with Dr. Martin L. West, October 30, 2010. Correspondence from Daniel Wallace to Josh McDowell, October 15, 2013. Thomas W. Allen, *Homeri Ilias* (1931; reprint, New York: Arno, 1979), 11–55. Personal correspondence with Dr. West, October 30, 2010. West added thirty-two early medieval manuscripts to Allen's 188 medieval manuscripts. See T. W. Allen, *Homer: The Origins and Transmissions* (Oxford). West also lists 142 Homerica papyri (glossaries, commentaries, *scholia minora*) and forty-seven witness papyri ("miscellaneous papyri and inscriptions in which verses of the *Iliad* are quoted"), ibid., 130.

2. Peter W. Flint, *The Dead Sea Scrolls* (Nashville: Abingdon, 2013), 38.

3. Quote from Dr. Scott Carroll speaking at the Discover the Evidence seminar, December 5, 2013, Plano, Texas.

4. Flint, *Dead Sea Scrolls*, 38.

5. Ibid., 39.

6. Ralph Earle, *How We Got Our Bible* (Grand Rapids: Baker, 1971), 48–49.

7. Flint, *Dead Sea Scrolls*, xx.

8. Ibid., xxi.

9. R. L. Harris, *Inspiration and Canonicity of the Bible* (Grand Rapids: Zondervan, 1957), 124.

10. Josh D. McDowell and Clay Jones, "The Bibliographical Test," December 5, 2013, adapted from an earlier article by Clay Jones, "The Bibliographical Test Updated," *Christian Research Journal* 35, no. 3 (2012).

11. Bill T. Arnold and Bryan E. Beyer, *Encountering the Old Testament* (Grand Rapids: Baker, 2008), 22.

12. See chapter 13, "Archaeology and Biblical Criticism," in Josh McDowell, *The New Evidence That Demands a Verdict* (Nashville: Thomas Nelson, 1999).

13. Pergamon Museum, Berlin: http://en.wikipedia.org/wiki/file: Pergamon_Museum_Berlin_2007085.jpg.

14. McDowell, *New Evidence*, 378.

15. Norman L. Geisler, *Baker Encyclopedia of Christian Apologetics* (Grand Rapids: Baker, 1998), 50–51.

16. Josh and Sean McDowell, *The Unshakable Truth* (Eugene, OR: Harvest House, 2010), 103.

17. Sean McDowell, "Bones and Dirt," *Apologetics Study Bible for Students* (Nashville: Broadman & Holman, 2009).

CHAPTER 12

1. Josh McDowell, *The New Evidence That Demands a Verdict* (Nashville: Thomas Nelson, 1999), 38.

2. Ibid., 38; and Josh D. McDowell and Clay Jones, "The Bibliographical Test," December 5, 2013, adapted from an earlier article by Clay Jones, "The Bibliographical Test Updated," *Christian Research Journal* 35, no. 3 (2012).

3. Joseph Angus, *The Bible Handbook* (London: Religious Tract Society, 1864), 56.

4. Norman L. Geisler and William E. Nix, *A General Introduction to the Bible* (Chicago: Moody, 1986), 430.

5. Ibid., 353–54.

6. Eusebius, *Ecclesiastical History III*, trans. C. F. Cruse, as quoted in Norman Geisler, *Baker's Encyclopedia of Christian Apologetics* (Grand Rapids: Baker, 1998), 39.

7. Irenaeus, *St. Irenaeus of Lyons: Against the Heresies*, trans. and annotated by Dominic J. Unger, with further revisions by John J. Dillon (New York: Paulist, 1992), 3.1.1.

8. Tacitus, *Annals*, in *The Annals and the Histories by Cornelius Tacitus*, vol. 15 of *Great Books of the Western World*, ed. Robert Maynard Hutchins (Chicago: William Benton, 1952), 44.

9. Suetonius, *Life of Claudius in The Twelve Caesars*, trans. Robert Graves, revised by Michael Grant (New York: Viking Penguin, 1979), 25.4.

10. Flavius Josephus, *The Antiquities of the Jews* (New York: Ward, Lock, Bowden, 1900), 20.9.1.

11. Pliny the Younger, *Letters*, trans. W. Melmoth, as quoted in Geisler, *Baker Encyclopedia of Christian Apologetics*, 10:96.

12. John Elder, *Prophets, Idols, and Diggers* (New York: Bobbs Merrill, 1960), 159–60; Joseph P. Free, *Archaeology and Bible History* (Wheaton, IL: Scripture Press, 1969), 285.

13. Elder, *Prophets, Idols, and Diggers*, 160.

14. Ibid., 259–60; Free, *Archaeology and Bible History*, 285.

15. Free, *Archaeology and Bible History*, 317.

16. F. F. Bruce, *The New Testament Documents: Are They Reliable?* (Downers Grove, IL: InterVarsity, 1964), 95; William F. Albright, *Recent Discoveries in Bible Lands* (New York: Funk and Wagnalls, 1955), 118.

17. F. F. Bruce, "Archaeological Confirmation of the New Testament," as cited in *Revelation and the Bible*, ed. Carl Henry (Grand Rapids: Baker, 1969), 325.

18. Ibid., 326.

19. Josh McDowell, *New Evidence*, 64.

CHAPTER 13

1. See chapters 13 and 17–21 in Josh McDowell, *The New Evidence That Demands a Verdict* (Nashville: Thomas Nelson, 1999).

2. McDowell, *New Evidence*, 376.

3. Ibid.

4. Harold L. Willmington, *Willmington's Bible Handbook* (Wheaton, IL: Tyndale, 1997), 889.

5. "Archaeology and Sources for Old Testament Background," *New Living Translation Study Bible* (Wheaton, IL: Tyndale, 2008), 8.

6. McDowell, *New Evidence*, 476–77.

7. F. F. Bruce, *The New Testament Documents: Are They Reliable?*, 6th ed. (Downers Grove, IL: InterVarsity, 1981), 42–43.

8. Ibid., 43.

9. Ibid.

10. W. F. Albright, *Recent Discoveries in Bible Lands* (New York: Funk and Wagnalls, 1955), 136.

11. William F. Albright, "Toward a More Conservative View," interview

in *Christianity Today*, January 18, 1963, 8.

12. W. F. Albright, *From the Stone Age to Christianity* (Baltimore: Johns Hopkins, 1940), 23.

13. John A. T. Robinson, *Redating the New Testament* (Eugene, OR: Wipf and Stock, 2000), 10.

14. Gleason L. Archer Jr., *Encyclopedia of Bible Difficulties* (Grand Rapids: Zondervan, 1982), 12.

CHAPTER 14

1. Pew Research Center, Washington, DC, Religion and Public Life Project, "The Global Religious Landscape," December 18, 2012, www.pewforum.org/2012/18/global-religious-landscape-exec.

2. Adapted from Josh and Sean McDowell, *77 FAQs about God and the Bible* (Eugene, OR: Harvest House, 2012), 206–8.

CHAPTER 15

1. As quoted by Sean McDowell, *Apologetics for a New Generation* (Eugene, OR: Harvest House, 2009), 141.

2. Adapted from Josh and Sean McDowell, *Experience Your Bible* (Eugene, OR: Harvest House, 2012), 37–48.

About the Author

Josh McDowell has been at the forefront of cultural trends and ground-breaking ministry for over five decades. He shares the essentials of the Christian faith in everyday language so that youth, families, churches, leaders, and individuals of all ages are prepared for the life of faith and the work of the ministry. This includes leveraging resources based on years of experiences, new technologies, and strategic partnerships. Since 1961, Josh has delivered more than 27,000 talks to over 25,000,000 people in 125 countries. He is the author or coauthor of 142 books, including More Than a Carpenter and New Evidence That Demands a Verdict, recognized by World Magazine as one of the top 40 books of the twentieth century. Josh's books are available in over 100 different languages. Josh and his wife, Dottie, are quick to acknowledge that after their love for the Lord, family is their greatest joy and top priority. They have been married for 43 years and have four wonderful children and ten beloved grandchildren. For more information, please visit www.josh.org.